So Far Disordered in Mind

RICHARD W. FOX

So Far Disordered in Mind

Insanity in California, 1870-1930

UNIVERSITY OF CALIFORNIA PRESS
Berkeley • *Los Angeles* • *London*

University of California Press
Berkeley and Los Angeles, California
University of California Press, Ltd.
London, England
Copyright © 1978 by
The Regents of the University of California
ISBN 0-520-03653-0
Library of Congress Catalog Card Number: 77-93479
Printed in the United States of America

1 2 3 4 5 6 7 8 9

For Diane, Rachel, and Christopher

Contents

Tables

Preface

This book is a study of the social and cultural meaning of insanity in California between 1870 and 1930, with special focus on the twentieth-century years. The whole period from the mid-nineteenth century to the 1920s was one of long-term change in medical and popular attitudes toward "mental illness" and in institutional modes of detention and treatment. But it was only after the turn of the century that the basic restructuring of cultural assumptions about mental deviance and social responses to mental deviants themselves became fully evident. The rise of the psychiatric profession to national prominence, the creation of urban psychopathic wards and "mental hygiene" clinics, the mounting conviction that minor mental disorders were nearly universal and that virtually anyone might require professional therapy at one time or another—these developments are central to the social history of the United States from 1905 to 1930.

Since the 1960s we have been witnessing a fitful challenge to the ideological and institutional network that had taken root by 1930 and had spread enormously after World War II. Psychiatry is today seriously divided from within and under attack from without, most significantly over the meaning and scientific status of the concept of "mental illness" itself, and over the legitimacy of invol-

xii   Preface

untary detention for those alleged to be mentally ill.
Lawyers, too, are split over the same issues. Government
officials are debating the utility of large hospitals for the
insane; some states, following the lead of California,
have closed hospitals and erected out-patient community
treatment centers in their place. Historians and sociologists are shedding light on the time-bound character of
contemporary assumptions about the insane by looking
at patterns of deviance and control since the Middle
Ages.

On the other hand, the therapeutic habit of mind—the
belief that virtually anyone may need professional help
to replenish depleted psychic resources, that individual
fulfillment may depend upon therapeutic intervention—
is much more firmly entrenched in American culture
today than it was one or two generations ago. The
mental health professions, including at least 28,000 psychiatrists and an estimated 325,000 other persons directly employed in caring for the "mentally ill"—a three-
fold increase since the 1950s—have developed a secure
cultural base. Their key assumptions have pervaded
everyday life. "It is now generally accepted," Karl Menninger wrote fifteen years ago, "that most people have
some degree of mental illness at some time, and may
have a degree of mental illness most of the time." The
mental health professions, it would seem, are becoming
the structurally diffuse but nonetheless established
"church" of twentieth-century society, whose priests, as
in some religions of old, command a sizable material
reward.[1]

The cost of treating the mentally ill has increased
tenfold over the last two decades, to about 17 billion
dollars annually. The provision of care for disturbed
persons has become a major industry, one that like all

1. *New York Times*, May 25, 1977, p. 16, and September 16, 1977, p. 16;
Karl Menninger, *The Vital Balance: The Life Process in Mental Health and
Illness* (New York, 1963), p. 33.

industries naturally seeks to extend the market and stimulate the demand for its product. It comes as no surprise that the President's Commission on Mental Health, in its public report of September 1977, judged "that many more Americans do have mental disturbances than was previously reported"; for seventy years mental hygienists have been sounding that same alarm. An estimated 15 to 20 percent of the population have "diagnosable mental disturbances," according to a National Institute of Mental Health study prepared for the Commission, and another 25 percent of Americans "suffer severe emotional stress."[2]

Since the beginning of the century, and especially since World War I, a rising proportion of Americans, apparently finding familial or religious counselors inadequate, have in fact turned to professionals for assistance. The mental health industry has both stimulated and grown in response to the demand for its services. Personal troubles, not new to the twentieth century, have come increasingly to be seen in a new way—as maladjustments or sicknesses that only properly certified authorities can understand and cure. Most psychological disturbances stem, in this view, from individual maladies or familial malfunctions for which neither society, other persons, nor the "patient" himself bears responsibility. That structural inequities in the social, economic, and political arena, or even individual moral failings, might be at the source of many such troubles is incompatible with the newly dominant viewpoint. Whereas in the nineteenth century insanity was commonly regarded as the product of a morally irresponsible existence—a result of willful disregard for widely shared moral norms— the contemporary mental patient is judged irresponsible only if she refuses to enter "voluntarily" the therapeutic relationship without which health is considered unat-

2. *New York Times*, May 25, 1977, p. 16, and September 16, 1977, p. 16.

tainable. The therapeutic society of the twentieth century combines a benign tolerance for "cooperative" disturbed persons with a potent, if largely implicit, buttressing of the socio-political status quo: psychic disturbance is seen as the product of individual or familial pathologies for which no one—and most certainly not the structures of the political economy—is ultimately to blame.

The goal of this book is to begin to sketch, in its wholeness, the ideological, institutional, and professional network in which judgments of normality and abnormality took place and were enforced before 1930—the years during which the "moral model" of deviant behavior was in the course of being displaced by the therapeutic model. This, it seems to me, ought to be the task of social history: to describe and analyze social development as a structural whole, with special attention to underlying forms of power, ideology, and human action that may not have been apparent to contemporaries. If this book makes a constructive start in the effort to illuminate the whole social network that gave insanity its particular meaning between 1870 and 1930, it will have achieved its goal. It is my hope that other scholars, particularly those with more background than I in the history of psychiatric thought and practice, will be able to draw upon this work in the course of writing still more thorough studies of the social history of insanity.

In an earlier incarnation this study was my doctoral dissertation at Stanford University. Professor Carl N. Degler, my adviser, helped me enormously with pointed, forthright suggestions on matters of conception, style, and organization. His enthusiasm for the project also provided a timely boost during the tedious months of data collection. To Barton J. Bernstein I am indebted for discussions over a period of years that gave me a new understanding of concepts central to this work—particularly the relationships between deviance, class, and ethnicity in American history.

I am grateful to a number of other scholars for discussions and letters over the last four years that forced me to clarify my approach to insanity and to social history in general. Gerald N. Grob, Nathan G. Hale, Jr., Christopher Lasch, and Christopher P. Wilson were especially generous with perceptive, if initially unsettling, criticisms that greatly strengthened the analysis. My intellectual debt to Professor Lasch's writings over the last decade is considerable. Although his latest book, *Haven in a Heartless World*—in part a forceful critique of the twentieth-century "helping professions"—appeared after this manuscript had been completed, I profited immensely from several of the earlier essays in which he sketched arguments further developed in the book. Professor Grob has on more than one occasion coaxed me gently into re-examining my interpretation. His repeated assistance has proved to me that scholars who disagree on major issues can for that very reason improve the quality of each other's work.

John C. Burnham, David Brion Davis, Estelle B. Freedman, Peter Dobkin Hall, Michael S. Hindus, Michael B. Katz, David M. Kennedy, Gerald L. Klerman, Carolyn C. Lougee, Terrence J. McDonald, Barbara G. Rosenkrantz, David B. Tyack, Stanton Wheeler, Allan M. Winkler, and the members of Yale University's Law and History Workshop also offered valuable comments on the manuscript or advice about the project. Regular conversations with Diane Fox about contemporary systems of detention and treatment sparked a number of insights that have found their way into this book. I am likewise grateful to one senior colleague who warned me quite seriously that I would be crazy to undertake a study of insanity since I had no credentials as a therapist; his unheeded advice alerted me to the pitfalls that await the unwary, non-professional student of medical matters.

The late Mrs. Elizabeth Avery of the San Francisco City and County Records Center permitted me to roam freely throughout the naturally refrigerated warehouse that the Center occupied until 1977. Her cooperation made possible the basic research on which this study is based. I also want to thank Dr. John Champlin of the Napa State Hospital, who accompanied me on a visit to the facility in 1974.

Financial assistance in the forms of a Whiting dissertation fellowship, a Stanford Post-Doctoral Fellowship in the Humanities, and a grant from Yale University's A. Whitney Griswold Faculty Research Fund, and bibliographical aid from librarians at the Stanford, University of California at Berkeley, San Francisco Public, California State, and Yale University libraries made the research and writing possible.

To my editor at the University of California Press, Alain L. Hénon, I am grateful for detecting promise in a doctoral dissertation and aiding me in a number of ways to bring it to publication. My thanks go also to my copy editor, Gene Tanke, for his remarkable attention to every detail of thought and expression, to Mrs. Jane E. Edwards and Mrs. Beverly Cederbaum for their meticulous typing of successive drafts, and to Natalie Callander for her care in proofreading the final manuscript.

Two other individuals deserve special mention for their role in earlier years in teaching me to think and to write: my father M. Bernard Fox, a writer and Socratic mind of the first order, and Michael Novak, the most stimulating teacher of my undergraduate years. Each conveyed an irresistible passion for question-asking— the starting point, as Aristotle held, not only of metaphysics but also of critical writing and thinking in general.

R. W. F.

1

Introduction:

The Social History of Insanity

For almost two decades psychiatric and sociological journals have been aflame with contentious disputes over the
"medical model" of "mental illness." The psychiatrists
Thomas Szasz and R. D. Laing, and sociologists Erving
Goffman and Thomas Scheff, have been at the forefront
of the effort to discredit the medical model. Far from
constituting an actual disease, they have argued, madness
is at bottom a culturally determined category for labeling
—and placing in confinement—certain particularly disturbing, often incomprehensible, types of social deviants.
Laing and his followers have in some of their work taken
the next logical step: madness can be considered a crea-
tive, intuitive probing of true reality.[1]

These critics of psychiatry and of mental institutions
have tended either to exaggerate the liberating character
of madness or to harp too exclusively on the "social
control" functions of psychiatry and mental hospitals,

1. Thomas Szasz, *The Myth of Mental Illness: Foundations of a Theory
of Personal Conduct* (New York, 1961), *Law, Liberty, and Psychiatry: An
Inquiry into the Social Uses of Mental Health Practices* (New York, 1963),
Psychiatric Justice (New York, 1965), and *The Manufacture of Madness: A
Comparative History of the Inquisition and the Mental Health Movement*
(New York, 1970); R. D. Laing, *The Politics of Experience* (New York,
1968); Erving Goffman, *Asylums: Essays on the Social Situation of Mental
Patients and Other Inmates* (New York, 1961); Thomas Scheff, *Being
Mentally Ill* (Chicago, 1966).

which are in some cases institutions of last resort for deeply troubled individuals incapable of caring for themselves. Moreover, as Christopher Lasch has pointed out, critics of "psychiatric justice" like Szasz are, despite their strictures against the use of the medical model to legitimize involuntary confinement, actually seeking to extend the therapeutic enterprise itself, by promoting the reliance of troubled individuals on psychiatric definitions, and therapeutic solutions, to their difficulties. In that respect they share more common ground with their opponents than they admit. The heated debate over the medical model obscures an underlying accord on the therapeutic model.[2]

Although Szasz, Laing, Scheff, Goffman, and others have not won their battle against the medical model of mental illness, they have performed the substantial service of alerting a wide readership to the undeniable sociocultural determinants of concepts of insanity, thereby helping to open a new frontier for historical research. Who in a particular society is defined as insane? What does that definition reveal to us about that society's cul-

2. Christopher Lasch, *Haven in a Heartless World: The Family Besieged* (New York, 1977), pp. 221-222, n. 28; Lasch, "Psychiatry: Call It Teaching or Call It Treatment," *Hastings Center Report* 5 (August 1975), 15-17. This is not the place to survey the complex arguments for and against the medical model. Suffice it to say that its defenders do not always define the model in an identical manner, and do not necessarily agree on the related but independent issue of whether and in which cases disturbed individuals may justifiably be detained against their will for treatment. Likewise the opponents of the medical model. Among the most compelling defenses of the model are Miriam Siegler and Humphrey Osmond, *Models of Madness, Models of Medicine* (New York, 1974), Alan A. Stone, *Mental Health and Law: A System in Transition* (Rockville, Md., 1975), and Peter Sedgwick, "Illness—Mental and Otherwise," *Hastings Center Studies* 1 (1973), 19-40. Among the most persuasive challenges to the medical model are Ronald Leifer, *In the Name of Mental Health* (New York, 1969), the essays in Thomas Scheff, ed., *Labelling Madness* (Englewood Cliffs, N.J., 1975), and Anthony Brandt, "Psychiatry and the Defense of Reality," *Soundings* 60 (Spring 1977), 108-122.

tural tensions, its conceptions of normality and of the meaning of human life? How are the insane treated? What does that treatment tell us about the culture's vision of social order, of medical healing, of moral regeneration?

Historians of the United States have just begun to venture into this uncharted territory. David Rothman and Gerald Grob have written broad studies of mental institutions in nineteenth-century America, and John C. Burnham, Nathan G. Hale, Jr., Norman Dain, and Charles Rosenberg have examined prevailing conceptions of mental disorder in the nineteenth and early twentieth centuries. Barbara Sicherman, in an unpublished work, has investigated the mental hygiene movement between 1880 and 1917.[3]

This study, while indebted to all of these researchers, takes a somewhat different course. The primary focus here is not upon mental institutions themselves or upon the thought of leading psychiatric authorities, but upon the social, institutional, and professional network within which thousands of deviant individuals were officially declared insane. Utilizing the insane commitment records of San Francisco City and County in the early

3. David J. Rothman, *The Discovery of the Asylum: Social Order and Disorder in the New Republic* (Boston, 1971); Gerald N. Grob, *Mental Institutions in America: Social Policy to 1875* (New York, 1973) and *The State and the Mentally Ill: A History of the Worcester State Hospital in Massachusetts, 1830-1920* (Chapel Hill, 1966); John C. Burnham, *Psychoanalysis and American Medicine: 1894-1918* (New York, 1967); Nathan G. Hale, Jr., *Freud and the Americans: The Beginnings of Psychoanalysis in the United States, 1876-1917* (New York, 1971); Norman Dain, *Concepts of Insanity in the United States, 1789-1865* (New Brunswick, N.J., 1964); Charles E. Rosenberg, *The Trial of the Assassin Guiteau: Psychiatry and Law in the Gilded Age* (Chicago, 1968); Barbara Sicherman, "The Quest for Mental Health in America, 1880-1917" (unpublished Ph.D. dissertation, Columbia University, 1967). Albert Deutsch, *The Mentally Ill in America: A History of Their Care and Treatment from Colonial Times to the Present* (New York, 1937), is dated but still useful.

twentieth century, I am attempting to elucidate the civil commitment process itself.

In the strictest sense the present study is not an examination of "mental illness" in early twentieth-century San Francisco, since most persons displaying symptoms of mental disturbance were never brought to court on insanity charges.[4] But it is impossible to grasp the social meaning of "insanity" in the early twentieth century without putting it in the context of the simultaneously expanding boundaries of the concept of "mental illness." The last chapter in particular will offer a still tentative analysis of the complex interrelationship between insanity and mental illness.

An analysis of individual case transcripts over a period of a quarter-century permits us to answer a number of critical questions about the commitment process. What types of people were officially judged insane? What brought them to the attention of the court, and what behavior did the court cite as evidence of insanity? What familial and professional groups, which institutional agencies, lay behind the commitment system? What can we conclude about the cultural meaning of insanity in industrial California? What can we establish about the social function of commitments for insanity in a major urban center in the early twentieth century?

II

As early as 1914 the Bureau of the Census reported that "there is relatively more insanity in cities than in country

4. Recent research has shown that despite the best efforts of the mental health professions, a very small proportion of those persons in the population with symptoms of mental illness—approximately one in fifteen—ever receives professional treatment, and a considerably smaller proportion ever undergoes an official examination for insanity. Benjamin Pasamanick, "A Survey of Mental Disease in an Urban Population: IV. An Approach to Total Prevalence Rates," *Archives of General Psychiatry* 5 (August 1961), 151-155; Scheff, *Being Mentally Ill*, pp. 47-50; David Mechanic, *Mental Health and Social Policy* (Englewood Cliffs, N.J., 1969), pp. 65-66.

districts and in large cities than in small cities"—a difference that persisted for both sexes and for all regions,
races, and nativity groups. Since at least that time, urban
sociologists have tried to explain the higher rates of
insane commitments in urban areas by pointing to the
allegedly distinctive stresses of urban living. "It is generally conceded," wrote the Chicago School's Nels Anderson and Eduard Lindeman in 1928, "that the large
city, with the strains and pressures of competition, tends
to exaggerate psychic abnormalities." In 1938 Louis
Wirth's seminal essay on "urbanism as a way of life"
summed up the prevailing view and gave it a more
sophisticated theoretical basis. Appropriating Durkheim's and Simmel's views on social disorganization and
urban anomie, Wirth asserted that "the 'schizoid' character of urban personality" might be explained by "the
multiplication of persons in a state of interaction under
conditions which make their contact as full personalities
impossible." Many studies of urban mental disorder—
such as Faris and Dunham's landmark "ecological" examination of Chicago in the 1930s—have explicitly or
implicitly assumed that the "life stress" of urban existence is distinctively harmful to psychic health.[5]

5. Department of Commerce, Bureau of the Census, *Insane and Feeble-
Minded in Institutions, 1910* (Washington D.C., 1914), pp. 49-53; Nels
Anderson and Eduard Lindeman, *Urban Sociology* (New York, 1928), p.
316; Louis Wirth, "Urbanism as a Way of Life," *American Journal of
Sociology* 44 (July 1938), 9; Robert E. L. Faris and H. Warren Dunham,
*Mental Disorders in Urban Areas: An Ecological Study of Schizophrenia
and Other Psychoses* (Chicago, 1939). Leo Srole *et al., Mental Health in the
Metropolis*, Book Two (New York, 1977) finally decisively challenges the
"antique presupposition of the superiority of rural mental health." Boyce
Rensberger, "Study Finds Urban Mental Health Better Than That in Rural
Areas" (interview with Leo Srole), *New York Times*, May 4, 1977, p. 1. See
also Bruce P. Dohrenwend's recent survey of studies on the difference
between rural and urban rates, which concludes that "functional psychoses"
are more prevalent in rural settings, while "neurosis" rates are higher in
cities. "Sociocultural and Social Psychological Factors in the Genesis of

This standard sociological view certainly seems plausible, especially since for over a century Americans have been accustomed to blaming "the city" for a wide range of social evils. Yet there is a twofold problem about this common approach to urban mental disorder. In the first place, sociologists have sometimes assumed that a higher rate of insane commitments or psychiatric treatments in a given locality signifies a higher rate of mental disturbances in that locality. Yet those facts may indicate only that an afflicted person in such an area is more likely to have access to treatment or to encounter the demand that he undergo it.[6] In the second place, the "individual anomie" perspective unjustifiably regards the city as an impersonal arena of purely "secondary relationships": urban dwellers are assumed to confront an unending series of faceless, utilitarian encounters. Mental illness, on this model, is the unfortunate, though understandable, response of certain individual organisms to an inhospitable environment.

But viewing the city as the battleground in the individual's solitary fight for psychic survival obscures two central components of urban existence. The city, first, is a center of ethnic, religious, and familial groups that have preserved for many residents some of the organic, personal relationships typically attributed to rural living alone.[7] Second, the city is a network of institutions that

---

Mental Disorders," *Journal of Health and Social Behavior* 16 (December 1975), 369-370.

6. John A. Clausen and Melvin L. Kohn provide the most comprehensive criticism of "The Ecological Approach in Social Psychiatry," in the *American Journal of Sociology* 60 (September 1954), 140-151. As they point out, "the probability of being labeled a 'case'" differs from one area to another (pp. 142-143).

7. On the survival and adaptation in urban centers of "organic" village relationships and roles, see, for example, Virginia Yans-McLaughlin, *Family and Community: Italian Immigrants in Buffalo, 1880-1930* (Ithaca, 1977). For the mid-twentieth-century, see, among others, Herbert Gans, *The Urban Villagers: Group and Class in the Life of Italian-Americans* (New York, 1965).

impinge upon individuals and kin groups at every point, even at the point of judging one person's behavior "sane" and another's "insane." There is little evidence to show that urbanization increased the rate at which people exhibited mental problems, any more than it increased the incidence of serious crime. But urbanization in industrailizing America did reduce middle-class tolerance for "unproductive," "inefficient" behavior, such as public drunkenness and loitering, and did promote the establishment of institutions and professions devoted to the control of deviant behavior.[8]

Studies of urban mental disorder must therefore consider the city as more than a dense field of atomized individuals. The city is also an arena of kin groups that often "contain" deviant behavior, of professions (especially medicine and social work) that define the boundaries of normality, and of specialized institutions (courts, police, hospitals) that detain and sometimes coerce the abnormal. Individuals develop and exhibit mental problems not in response to an abstract environment, but in contact with relatives, acquaintances, and official authorities who consider their behavior "disturbed." It is in this context of group life and of institutional and professional power—power both to delineate norms and to coerce the abnormal—that we must study the phenomenon of madness in urban America.

III

In early and mid-nineteenth century America, as David Rothman, Gerald Grob, and others have shown, the construction of asylums designed to "cure," rather than simply confine, the insane and other deviants became a cornerstone of social policy. A phalanx of reformers, appalled by the growing threat of deviant behavior to

8. Herbert Goldhamer and Andrew Marshall, *Psychosis and Civilization* (Glencoe, Ill., 1953); Roger Lane, "Crime and the Industrial Revolution: British and American Views," *Journal of Social History* 7 (Spring 1974), 287-303.

social order, and convinced that cures would follow from the patient intervention of middle-class humanitarians like themselves, persuaded state legislatures to erect scores of imposing edifices for the detention and rehabilitation of the mad, the criminal, and the poor. By mid-century "progressive" states no longer intermingled these groups in all-purpose almshouses, but carefully segregated them into insane asylums, prisons, and almshouses for the poor.

Rothman's thesis that the discovery of the asylum occurred in response to the social disorder of the antebellum period, that reformers pushed the new institutions as a means of knitting together the frayed fabric of Jacksonian society, has been strongly criticized. It neglects the European counterparts and antecedents of American asylums, and ignores the religious perfectionism that lay behind the institutional reformers' support for institutionalization. But the most fundamental criticism of *The Discovery of the Asylum* has been directed to its "social-control" stance: its contention that the "asylum"—which signifies for Rothman not just mental hospitals but also almshouses, orphan asylums, penitentiaries, and reformatories—"represented an effort to insure the cohesion of the community" in the face of "unprecedented dangers and unprecedented opportunities."[9]

It is important to focus in some detail upon Rothman's use of the "social control" paradigm, because this

9. Rothman, *Discovery of the Asylum*, p. xviii; reviews of *Discovery of the Asylum* by Gerald Grob, in *Reviews in American History* 1 (March 1973), 43-52, by Jacques M. Quen, in *Journal of Psychiatry and Law* 2 (Spring 1974), 105-122, and by James Banner, *Journal of Interdisciplinary History* 5 (Summer 1974), 167-174; Christopher Lasch, "The Origins of the Asylum," *The World of Nations: Reflections on American History, Politics, and Culture* (New York, 1974), pp. 315-316. See also Grob's thoughtful reflections on "Rediscovering Asylums: The Unhistorical History of the Mental Hospital," *Hastings Center Report* 7 (August 1977), 33-41, especially n. 37.

study is both indebted to it and highly critical of it. His book *The Discovery of the Asylum* performed the salutary function of strongly challenging the common scholarly view in which the spread of asylums constituted "progress," and was attributable to the growth of "humanitarian concern" among antebellum reformers. In addition, his study rightly insisted upon the manifold ties that linked different types of institutions often treated in isolation. My criticism of his work is meant not to belittle his real achievement, but to suggest a way of advancing beyond the use of "social control" as a basic interpretive device.[10]

The Discovery of the Asylum exhibits a number of key flaws that mark many social-control interpretations of nineteenth-century America. It is not only that "social control," like the "status anxiety" of a decade ago, has been so overused that it is frequently applied carelessly, or that the "order-disorder" formula has become trite through excessive use. It is rather that even the most sophisticated social-control arguments tend to fall into one or more of three mistakes: (1) they reify the "controllers" to the point that they become either a homogeneous elite, or, in Rothman's case, indistinguishable from society as a whole; (2) they assume that institutions are imposed by that elite or that society upon a passive, malleable "lower" class; and (3) they exaggerate the novelty of nineteenth-century perceptions of disorder and in some cases of nineteenth-century institutions themselves.[11]

10. The following paragraphs draw upon my review article "Beyond Social Control: Institutions and Disorder in Bourgeois Society," *History of Education Quarterly* 16 (Summer 1976), 203-207.

11. Other significant examples of "social-control" interpretations are Michael Katz, *The Irony of Early School Reform: Educational Innovation in Mid-Nineteenth Century Massachusetts* (Cambridge, 1968); Stanley Schultz, *The Culture Factory: Boston Public Schools, 1789-1860* (New York, 1973); Anthony Platt, *The Child Savers: The Invention of Delinquency* (Chicago, 1969); and Allan Horlick, *Country Boys and Merchant Princes: The Social*

In Rothman's analysis, the disorder of Jacksonian society gives rise to a generalized movement to restore order. Social control appears to be no more in the interest of one social group than of another; it is a mysteriously diffuse movement toward equilibrium characterizing an entire society—a society that has slipped, for reasons that remain unclear, into a temporary state of disequilibrium. Control is re-established in his account by "society" itself—with the apparently disinterested help of the asylum reformers. Rothman thus manages to steer clear of the basic question of whether institutionalization served the interests of any group or class. Moreover, he tends to use the asylum reformers' own claims of unprecedented social upheaval as his primary evidence for the existence of disorder—without asking whether it was in the professional self-interest of such reformers to exaggerate the extent of the upheaval in order to help loosen the purse-strings of state legislators.

One diffuse group did nevertheless lose more than the others in, Rothman's account: the deviant population itself. Although Rothman resists the temptation to romanticize the "victims," he still tends to view them as the helpless tools of the reformers' schemes for restoring order. He assumes a rigid separation between, on the one hand, the social world of the deviants, and on the other hand, the broader society within which the movement for "control" originates. But what this standpoint overlooks is the fact that in many cases, lower-class or working-class families in the nineteenth century were themsevles instrumental in bringing about the confinement of their own disturbed or disturbing relatives and neighbors. The insane, the poor, the delinquent, and the criminal were frequently not just a threat to the value system of the wider community—of the middle class and its

---

Control of Young Men in New York (Lewisburg, Pa., 1975), to mention only a few.

reformers—but also a formidable burden to their own families and neighborhoods. Those families and neighborhoods may have welcomed the extension of government control in the fight against forms of disorder that afflicted them as much as, or more than, any other group. Particularly in the case of the insane, the financial burden of caring for even partially disabled family members must have been too great for many families to bear. State institutions to which the old or unproductive or delinquent could be committed undoubtedly appeared to such families—though perhaps not to the deviants themselves—as regrettable but indispensable necessities.[12]

Rothman's essential point, that official American policy on the management of deviance shifted markedly in the Jacksonian period, is beyond dispute. Reformers and legislators at the state level began to commit massive resources to the building and staffing of "bastilles" for the sequestering and reforming of a wide range of deviants. But Rothman draws the unwarranted conclusion that institutionalization as a "preferred solution" to the problem of deviance was an innovation of the nineteenth century. A careful reading of Michel Foucault's *Madness and Civilization*—which he cites as "fascinating and suggestive" but abruptly brushes aside as unsatisfactory— ought to have put him on guard. For what Foucault makes clear is that the initial "discovery" of the asylum —considered as an official institution for the sequestering of deviants—was actually a development of the seventeenth century, the age, in Foucault's phrase, of the "great confinement."

There is some evidence in Rothman's own account of the American case that supports Foucault's interpreta-

---

12. Andrew T. Scull, in a study of English asylums, has made this point forcefully. "Madness and Segregative Control: The Rise of the Insane Asylum," *Social Problems* 24 (February 1977), 348. So has Steven Schlossman in his book on delinquency in Milwaukee, *Love and the American Delinquent* (Chicago, 1977), *passim*.

tion, but he minimizes that evidence in order to argue that institutionalization in Jacksonian America represented a radical break with the past. He tries needlessly to locate in the early nineteenth century both the initial appearance of institutions and their later expansion and differentiation as a matter of official state policy. His own research makes clear that institutional care arose in urban centers in the seventeenth and eighteenth centuries—not just as a matter of "last resort," but at least in some cases as a matter of preferred social policy.

The New York authorities, for example, enacted a measure in 1735 "ordering all the poor into the almshouse." Rothman submits that their plan ultimately failed, but the question is not whether the plan succeeded but whether it represented the officially preferred solution. Furthermore, the Boston almshouse opened in 1664, and by the mid-eighteenth century (the only period for which records are extant) it housed about one-fourth of all the Boston poor receiving relief—or roughly 250 out of a total of about 1000 persons. Rothman might have explained these data by arguing that in colonial America institutionalization was the preferred solution only in the case of transients. But he assumes, perhaps incorrectly in view of recent research, that transient strangers did not constitute a large-scale social problem in late colonial society. He therefore denies that institutions for the containment of deviants played an important social role prior to 1830—a position that allows him to posit a generalized Jacksonian urge to control disorder as the explanation for their "discovery."[13]

But if institutions for the management of deviance were in fact being established in the seventeenth and eighteenth centuries—not only in Europe but in America

13. Rothman, *Discovery of the Asylum*, pp. 38-41. On the extent of transiency in colonial America, and institutional efforts to control transient deviants, see Douglas Jones, "The Strolling Poor: Transiency in Eighteenth-Century Massachusetts," *Journal of Social History* 8 (Spring 1975), 28-54.

as well—how can we best account for their emergence? Foucault's perspective offers a suggestive framework. Underlying the rise of institutions, he argues, was a shift in cultural attitudes toward deviance that had become widespread by the end of the seventeenth century. Deviant behavior, previously regarded as part of the order of things—and in the case of madness sometimes seen as a mysterious form of participation in the world of spirit—came to be associated with a willful lack of productivity, a failure to contribute labor to the "marketplace." "Confinement," writes Foucault, "was an institutional creation peculiar to the seventeenth century. It acquired from the first an importance that left it no rapport with imprisonment as practiced in the Middle Ages. . . . It marked a decisive event: the moment when madness was perceived . . . [as] incapacity for work." This bourgeois value system—the indispensable precondition for the spread of the market economy and the subsequent growth of cities and the onset of industrialization—promoted the sequestering of individuals who represented a real or imagined threat to that world view.[14]

The discovery of the asylum occurred not when state officials decided to finance an expansion of institutional care in the nineteenth century, but when bourgeois cultural attitudes took hold of burgeoning urban centers—as well as rural areas being brought into the market economy—in the seventeenth and eighteenth centuries. It was then that the poor, the insane, and the criminal began to be seen as irresponsible, willfully negligent, a threat to the public order that only institutional detention could counter.[15]

---

14. Michel Foucault, *Madness and Civilization: A History of Insanity in the Age of Reason*, trans. Richard Howard (New York, 1965), p. 61. See also Lasch, "The Origins of the Asylum," p. 17.

15. Andrew T. Scull gives extended treatment to this theme in "Madness and Segregative Control," pp. 337-351 (reprinted with minor alterations as Chapter Two of his book *Decarceration: Community Treatment and the*

The "social-control" perspective flattens out these vital structural developments by positing an abstract conflict between a group of controllers and their victims, and then by moralistically upbraiding the controllers for their alleged inclination to dominate. But while rejecting social control as an interpretive tool, it is important to preserve the kernel of truth its proponents are seeking to express. The development of Western capitalist society did not proceed equally in the interests of all; many deviants were incarcerated not because they were burdens to their families but because their life-styles offended middle-class sensibilities; reformers were motivated not only by humanitarian concern, but also, and simultaneously, by their professional self-interest in the expansion of "welfare" institutions. While moving beyond social control we must not lose sight of the realities of class, power, and ideology that formed the boundaries of the social world in which all men—whether they were aware of it or not—lived out their lives.

IV

By the late nineteenth century, the indefinite commitment of disturbed, troublesome individuals to large custodial asylums was standard practice in the United States. The therapeutic optimism of the first generation of antebellum "alienists" had become muted; asylum superintendents no longer claimed that their immediate object was to cure insanity. They now administered institutions of such size, made up of patients from class and ethnic backgrounds so different from their own, that "moral treatment"—the key to the reported cures of the early nineteenth century—was impossible. The emerging theoretical correlate of this institutional impasse was the

---

Deviant—A Radical View, Englewood Cliffs, N.J., 1977), and in "Museums of Madness: The Social Organization of Insanity in Nineteenth Century England" (unpublished Ph.D. dissertation, Princeton University, 1974).

belief that insanity was an organic, not a "functional," impairment; it was an incurable affliction for which custodial detention was the only conceivable "treatment."[16]

In the early twentieth century, medical opinion and popular attitudes were in flux. A functional conception of mental disease re-emerged, one that traced the roots of disorder either to the unconscious, as in psychoanalysis, or, more commonly, to problems of living resulting from a combination of environmental evils and hereditary taint.[17] While in the late nineteenth century "insanity" and "mental disease" tended to be interchangeable labels for a mysterious organic disease, the terms now began to acquire new, distinguishable meanings. "Mental disease," or more commonly "mental illness," became an umbrella concept that covered both "insanity" and a wide range of relatively minor mental and nervous disorders—disturbances increasingly viewed as both commonplace and transitory. Once again, physicians displayed an optimistic spirit; "mental illness," if treated promptly by trained professionals, could in many cases be cured. The institutional counterpart of this emerging conception was the psychopathic ward—an urban treatment center which, its enthusiastic proponents claimed, would restore the mental health of the ever-increasing number of moderately disturbed sufferers.[18] On the other hand, "insanity" came to connote the more serious, intractable afflictions, which had in some cases an organic

16. Rothman, *Discovery of the Asylum*, pp. 109-154, 265-295; Grob, *Mental Institutions in America*, pp. 174-256; Dain, *Concepts of Insanity in the United States*, pp. 204-209; Hale, *Freud and the Americans*, pp. 47-97.

17. Hale, *Freud and the Americans*, pp. 151-176, 434-461.

18. Such professional enthusiasm appears to arise whenever a self-conscious group of professional reformers seeks to justify, and obtain public financing for, institutional innovations, whether they be hospitals, prisons, schools, or other new establishments. See Katz, *The Irony of Early School Reform*, and W. David Lewis, *From Newgate to Dannemora: The Rise of the Penitentiary in New York, 1796-1848* (Ithaca, 1965).

etiology, but which usually stemmed from some unfortunate mixture of environment and heredity. The "insane" were those "mentally ill" persons who were completely incapable of functioning in the community, who were unable or unwilling to cooperate in their treatment, and who therefore still required indefinite confinement in locked asylums.

The chapters that follow will attempt to shed new light on this period of restructuring in popular and medical assumptions and practices and in institutional modes of detention and treatment. Chapters Two and Three will examine the institutional and ideological developments that underlay the commitment process in California in the late nineteenth and early twentieth centuries. Chapter Four, Five, and Six will focus on the insane of San Francisco—the more than 12,000 individuals committed for insanity between 1906 and 1929. A statistical study of their case records permits us to generalize about the common "routes" the insane took to the asylum (Chapter Four), about the social backgrounds of the insane (Chapter Five), and about the behavior cited by the court as evidence of insanity (Chapter Six). Chapter Seven will place the San Francisco commitment process in the broader context of the developing meanings of "insanity" and "mental illness" in the early twentieth century.

2

Insanity in the Promised State: Ideologies and Institutions, 1870-1930

Historians are in uncharacteristic agreement about the actual function of insane hospitals in late nineteenth- and early twentieth-century America: the asylums were, and were commonly considered by observers of the time, to be custodial rather than therapeutic institutions. Leaving aside the important question of whether and in what way an institution in any period can rightly be termed "therapeutic," California hospitals for the insane still differed from eastern institutions in a fundamental way.[1] Whereas many eastern hospitals were thought by contemporary observers and subsequent historians to have "declined" from therapy to custody, California asylums underwent no such apparent transition. From their very beginnings in the 1850s they were clearly understood to be not simply treatment facilities for the mentally disturbed, but also detention facilities for "imbeciles, dotards, idiots, drunkards, simpletons, fools," for "the aged, the vagabond, the helpless." The efforts of superintendents in the 1850s to establish a humanitarian "moral treatment" regime—modeled after earlier eastern efforts—

1. A large sociological and medical literature has accumulated on the question of "therapeutic" institutions. See, for example, the essays in Richard H. Price and Bruce Denner, eds., *The Making of a Mental Patient* (New York, 1973), and the brief, provocative assessment in Christopher Lasch, "The Origins of the Asylum," *The World of Nations* (New York, 1974), pp. 3-17.

were futile from the start, since their patient populations were both too large and composed of such a wide
variety of deviants. In California "custody" was paramount from the start.[2]

From the 1870s to the 1920s California had the highest rate of insane commitments in the nation. In 1870,
according to the federal census, one in every 489 Californians was insane, compared with a national average
of one to 1031. Only Vermont had a higher rate, with one
to 458, but a substantially higher proportion of Vermont's insane were cared for at home. By 1880, California was the clear leader, with one in every 345 residents insane according to the census. Though the census
figures were widely believed even at the time to be
highly inaccurate, all commentators agreed that California had more insane commitments in proportion to
population than any other state.[3] Disagreement arose
only in accounting for that statistic. Did it prove that
Californians were actually "the craziest people in the
world"—as apparently many Americans, and even for-

2. Dr. W. H. Mays, "Report of the Medical Superintendent," *Thirty-
Third and Thirty-Fourth Annual Reports of the Insane Asylum of the State
of California at Stockton* (Sacramento, 1886), pp. 15-16; Dr. John W.
Robertson, "Prevalence of Insanity in California," *American Journal of
Insanity* 60 (July 1903), 81. Michael T. Savino and Alden B. Mills, "The Rise
and Fall of Moral Treatment in California Psychiatry: 1852-1870," *Journal
of the History of the Behavioral Sciences* 3 (October 1967), 359-369,
presents little evidence that moral treatment was any more than an idea—
an idea whose time had passed—at Stockton State Hospital in the 1850s. On
moral treatment itself, see Grob, *Mental Institutions in America*, pp. 180-
181.

3. Department of the Interior, Census Office, *Ninth Census*, Vol. II,
Vital Statistics (Washington, 1872), p. 473; *Ninth Census, Statistics of
Population* (Washington, 1872), p. 3; *Tenth Census, Report on the Defec-
tive, Dependent and Delinquent Classes* (Washington, 1888), p. XII; Dr. E.
T. Wilkins, *Insanity and Insane Asylums* (Sacramento, 1872), pp. 200-201;
Biennial Report of the Trustees of the Napa State Asylum for the Insane
(Sacramento, 1892), p. 11. In 1890 Nevada had a higher rate—one out of
250 residents to California's one in 323—but Nevada's rate was based on a

eigners, believed?[4] Or did it signify simply that California courts committed a wider variety of individuals than those of other jurisdictions?

In the late nineteenth century California hospital superintendents oscillated between the two explanations. Dr. E. T. Wilkins, California's foremost alienist in the 1870s, was typically ambivalent. In a major report on "insanity and insane asylums" in the United States and Europe, he argued that the high rate of insanity in California stemmed from two distinct facts. First, "her citizens have been exposed to a greater number of causes by which this malady is developed." Second, California "is perhaps the only State in the Union, if not the only Government in the world, that has never refused admission to a single

---

statistically insignificant total of 183 insane persons. Census Office, *Report on the Insane, Feeble-Minded, Deaf and Dumb, and Blind in the United States at the Eleventh Census* (Washington, 1895), p. 9. One might suspect that since insanity was almost always an adult phenomenon, California's consistently high rate might be explained by a disproportionate number of adults in the state's population. But California's proportion of adults over 20 (60.1 percent in 1880, 63.5 in 1890) was comparable to eastern states like New York (58.6 percent in 1880, 61.4 percent in 1890) and Massachusetts (61.9 percent in 1880, 64.0 percent in 1890), and those states had consistently fewer insane residents *per capita*. What also strikingly distinguishes California from the other states that committed the highest absolute numbers of insane in the late nineteenth century is the high percentage of its insane committed to state hospitals. In 1880, for example, of the 2503 insane Californians reported by the Census, 2010 (80.3 percent) were in state hospitals, while only 2.7 percent were in almshouses and 16.5 percent living at home. By contrast, in New York state 57.5 percent of the 14,055 insane were in state hospitals, 11.2 percent in almshouses, and 31 percent at home; in Massachusetts, 60 percent of the 5,127 insane were in state hospitals, 9.2 percent in almshouses, and 30.4 percent at home. No other state came close to California's proportion of hospitalized insane. *Tenth Census, Report on the Defective, Dependent, and Delinquent Classes*, p. 39.

4. Dr. E. T. Wilkins, "Report of the Resident Physician," *Report of the Board of Trustees of the Napa State Asylum for the Insane* (Sacramento, 1877), pp. 21-22; Dr. A. M. Gardner, "California and the Insane," *Proceedings*, American Medico-Psychological Association (New York, 1898), pp. 341-350; Robertson, "Prevalence of Insanity in California," 75.

person who has sought to enter her asylum"—a decep-
tive formulation, since in the 1870s, as in the early
twentieth century, it was rarely the insane person himself, but rather various petitioners, physicians, and judges
who sought the confinement. "It is a well-known fact,"
Dr. Wilkins concluded, "that among those received there
have been and still are many citizens of other countries,
who have not claimed California as a home, but who
have come here hoping to better their fortunes and
enrich themselves at her expense, and then return to
their own homes and country; but failing to realize their
dreams of wealth, give way to despondency, break down
in health, or enter upon a course of reckless dissipation
that leads them to insanity and to our asylum."[5] California had such a high rate of insanity both because its
social life was particularly unsettling, and because
state policy encouraged the commitment of all who
"sought" it.

Other medical authorities also invoked the popular
view of recent California history to explain the first
alleged fact, namely, that the California environment
promoted mental disorder. From "the discovery of our
marvelous gold fields," claimed the State Board of Health
in 1873, "the enterprising and the adventurous of every
country, race, religion, and character have flocked hither
to form the most cosmopolitan State in the world. On a
people of such heterogeneous elements, exposed to all the
evils incident to change of climate, habits, and modes of
life, isolated, without sympathy, and deprived of all home
influences, the shock attendant upon the sudden acquisi-
tion of wealth, with its unbounded hopes, its sudden
reverses and short-lived triumphs, is well-calculated to
break some link in reason's chain, and throw into confusion even the best balanced properties of mind." If one
also considered "the speculative and gambling spirit in

5. Wilkins, *Insanity and Insane Asylums*, p. 209.

our community" and the "prevailing vice of intemperance . . . unequaled in any part of the world, it is not surprising that insanity has increased at such a fearful rate."[6]

According to this view, adjusting to California required adapting not only to a new climate, genuinely unsettled social conditions, and in many cases to solitude —all experiences common to other frontiers—but also to the particularly unsettling shock of rapidly acquiring and losing wealth. Such an experience was proposed as typical for new residents to the state. In the words of Dr. George Shurtleff, the superintendent of the state's single asylum in 1875, "the shock of transplantation, separation from family and friends, disappointments, disastrous enterprises, sudden reverses of fortune, intemperance, fast living, and an unsettled condition of life, are the chief causes of mental disorder on the Pacific Coast."[7] The fact that the majority of the insane even in the 1870s were by occupation either laborers or housewives—not miners, speculators, or merchants—apparently did not suggest that the argument was overstated. In fact, to exaggerate the case was in the self-interest of the asylum physicians —especially in the early 1870s, when the state's single

6. *Second Biennial Report of the State Board of Health of California* (Sacramento, 1873), pp. 66. (Hereafter the Board's reports will be cited in this form: 2 *Cal. St. Bd. Health* 1873.) In the same year Dr. Wilkins expressed the paradoxical view that "it is devoutly to be hoped that the use of poisonous alcoholic compounds, that the ingenious contrivances of civilization have furnished to man in such tempting forms, will decrease with the increase in quantity and improvement in quality of our native wines." "Insanity in California," *Transactions of the Medical Society of the State of California* 3 (1873), 137.

7. Dr. G. A. Shurtleff, "The Insane, and Why So Many," 3 *Cal. St. Bd. Health* 1875, p. 65. As early as 1852 the *Daily Alta California*, seeking to explain the "surprising[ly] . . . great number of insane persons" in San Francisco, pointed to "the fact that so many come to this country with the expectation of making a lasting fortune in one day, and are sorely disappointed when they discover that energy and industry are required to accomplish their object." "Lunatics," March 6, 1852, p. 2.

facility at Stockton was overflowing with patients. Fostering the view that Californians were distinctly liable to fall victim to insanity might well help convince legislators to allocate continually larger sums for the construction of new asylums and the expansion of old ones.

Yet the same medical authorities were aware that the "liberal" state commitment policy was also responsible for swelling the ranks of the insane. In Dr. Shurtleff's words, "nearly every form of mental infirmity and impairment, in persons who are indigent and become burdensome, is called insanity, and the subjects thereof are committed to the Insane Asylum. Hence we have counted as insane mere simpletons, epileptics who are simply troublesome, senile dements, methomaniacs [those with a craving for alcohol], and so forth. Take from the insane these classes, who in Europe and the older States would be provided for in other public institutions . . . and the sum total of insanity now ascribed to California would be materially reduced."[8] The state government, in the superintendent's view, had mistakenly—though surely from humanitarian motives—assumed the whole responsibility for sheltering all helpless and irresponsible individuals and had further erred in grouping them all in an insane asylum, rather than providing a state poorhouse for harmless or aged indigents.

Throughout the nineteenth century these two medical viewpoints coexisted. California—the uniquely unsettled society—promoted more insanity than other states, and the state government unwisely promoted the further inflation of the commitment rate. Perhaps the superintendents consciously or unconsciously exaggerated the chaotic character of California social life in an effort to mobilize public and legislative support for their work. But it also seems possible that up to the end of the century Californians in general subscribed to the view that their culture was particularly unsettled. It may even

8. Shurtleff, "The Insane and Why So Many," p. 66.

have been more "disordered" than other frontiers, through the combined effects of the state's population explosion and its unique "gold fever." But even if the general perception of unusual disorder did not correspond to social reality, that perception may have made California legislators more willing than those of other states to provide for a higher proportion of insane commitments. To construct and encourage easy access to asylums might seem then to be a way of "civilizing" the state—by treating and sometimes curing individuals who had succumbed to its overwhelming pressures. Moreover, large expenditures for the insane might have seemed a means of increasing the state's prestige in the rest of the nation as a leader in progressive reform. Such at least was the opinion of the State Board of Health. "Of all the eleemosynary institutions . . . so creditable to the enlightened humanity of our State, none have received so much consideration from our Legislature, or required so great an expenditure of the public treasure, as our State Lunatic Asylum."[9]

By the turn of the century the ambivalence characteristic of medical explanations of rising insanity rates had given way to a more unified picture. Perhaps as a result of the fading into memory of the pioneering generation, the image of California as a uniquely unsettling environment—promoting and then dashing unbounded hopes— appears to have disappeared. The new viewpoint took it for granted that California was no more unsettling than any other industrial state. Nothing inherent in the California environment gave rise to insanity. Rather, charity administrators, asylum officials, and other physicians argued, large numbers of persons who already had financial or medical difficulties in other localities tended disproportionately to come to California, seeking either work or health or both. Since they were predisposed to breakdown before arrival, they could be expected to in-

9. 2 *Cal. St. Bd. Health* 1873, p. 66.

flate California's rate of insanity within a short period of time. "The large numbers who come to California annually in search of health," wrote the State Board of Charities and Corrections in its first report in 1905, "contribute largely to the ranks of mental defectives. . . . California, by reason of geographical location, naturally receives and retains more than her share of transient defectives, both from her sister States and from foreign countries."[10] In 1908 the State Commission in Lunacy— the official agency created in 1887 to manage the asylums —reported that it had undertaken a serious effort to deport "alien and non-resident insane," who were in large measure responsible for the overcrowded conditions in the state's hospitals.[11]

In explaining the high rate of insanity in California, this newly prevailing viewpoint managed to put the blame on other states and countries—which had produced the "defectives"—while at the same time praising not only the state's climate but its generous willingness to care for all those who broke down after arrival. In 1903—when the rate had risen to one insane person in every 260 residents—Dr. John Robertson of the prestigious (private) Livermore Sanitarium, and a former state hospital physician, gave vigorous expression to this standpoint in the national journal of the hospital superintendents. After granting that "statistics certainly show that California not only leads the other States, but is well

10. *First Biennial Report of the State Board of Charities and Corrections* (Sacramento, 1905), p. 36. (Hereafter cited as 1 *St. Bd. Char. and Corr.* 1905.)

11. *Sixth Biennial Report of the State Commission in Lunacy* (Sacramento, 1908), p. 23. (Hereafter cited in the form 6 *St. Comm. Lun.* 1908.) Interestingly, the State Board offered the same explanation for the overcrowding of the state prisons, which had "a much greater number of criminals in proportion to . . . population than most States of the union"— both because of climate and since, "being a seaboard state, the criminal driftwood that floats in from other countries finds its first lodgement here." 2 *St. Bd. Char. and Corr.* 1906, p. 33.

in advance of the most civilized countries of Europe" in its rate of insane commitments, Robertson asserted that the high rate was a sign of a superior civilization. A "high insane ratio" did not imply a "nervously bankrupt" state; it meant rather that Californians gave "unstintingly, that the lives of these unfortunates may not only be rendered bearable, but in many ways pleasant." Such liberal provisions for the insane demonstrated that California was not only "civilized, but, to the highest degree, humanized."[12]

The implications of the newly dominant explanation of California's high rate of insanity were far-reaching. For if California continued to attract such a great proportion of defectives, the state's insane hospitals would at some point be unable to accommodate the flow; even the corridors, floors, and basements, where patients already slept in large numbers, would be totally filled.[13] Before 1912 state hospital officials could take some comfort in the fact that however great the increase in insane commitments, the general population of the state was growing even faster. In 1908 they estimated that California's population had risen 33 percent since the turn of the century, compared to a rise in hospital admissions of 24 percent. In 1910, their revised estimate showed a 60 percent jump in the state's population since 1900, compared to a 35 percent increase in hospital commitments.[14]

But beginning in 1912 a new sense of alarm took hold of hospital and charity administrators. The biennial period from 1910 to 1912 showed the largest proportional increase in the insane population since the turn of the century. Between 1910 and 1914, while the state's popu-

12. Robertson, "Prevalence of Insanity in California," pp. 75-77.

13. "Inhuman Treatment of the Insane," *San Francisco Call*, March 12, 1911, p. 30. Of the 6,254 patients in state hospitals in June 1908, 761 (over 12 percent) were sleeping on floors (401) or in basements or corridors (360). 3 *St. Bd. Char. and Corr.* 1908, pp. 66, 188.

14. 6 *St. Comm. Lun.* 1908, p. 9; 7 *St. Comm. Lun.* 1910, p. 11.

lation, according to their estimate, had risen by 15 percent, the insane population had risen by 22 percent. And between 1910 and 1917 the insane population grew by 46 percent, compared to a population increase of 26 percent. Similarly, according to the State Commission in Lunacy, the total United States population increased by 12 percent and the national insane population by 25 percent in those same eight years. By 1912, state officials reported, many hospital wards—designed to handle 40 patients each—housed 120. Each attendant was responsible for an average of 15 patients—a larger ratio than in other states—and had not only to work six and one-half days a week, but to sleep in the ward, and be on call, each night. One superintendent was actually discharging "from 5 to 10 patients each month who ought not to be discharged, because he has to make room for new patients coming in."[15]

California's asylum system—which had in the late nineteenth century been expected to help stabilize an unsettled society, and, by the turn of the century, to care for and control the thousands of incoming transient defectives—had reached a crisis by the second decade of the twentieth century. In the opinion of the hospital superintendents themselves, public and legislative support for still more asylums—by now there were five—would not be forthcoming.[16] As a result, new policies for handling defective deviants—proposals designed to reduce the population of the insane hospitals—emerged at the state level. The enactment of deportation, parole, and probation programs was one part of the new approach, although the numbers they affected were quite small. The two most significant policy innovations were

15. 5 *St. Bd. Char. and Corr.* 1912, pp. 30-33, 87; 9 *St. Comm. Lun.* 1914, p. 10; 11 *St. Comm. Lun.* 1918, p. 64.
16. Dr. A. W. Hoisholt, "Discussion," *Proceedings*, Third California State Conference of Charities and Corrections (Whittier, 1904), pp. 66-67. (Hereafter cited as 3 *Cal. St. Conf. Char. and Corr.* 1904.)

the campaign for urban psychopathic wards, to be discussed in the next chapter, and the crusade to sterilize the defective—a program that carried the asylum's "social-control" function to a new extreme.

II

Sterilization of the insane caught on in California as it did in no other state. First made possible by the state legislature in 1909, "asexualization" was progressively extended to cover more individuals by amendments of 1913 and 1917. The 1913 measure specified that sterilization could be performed "with or without the consent of the patient." The 1917 act extended the procedure beyond those "afflicted with hereditary insanity or incurable chronic mania or dementia" to all "those suffering from perversion or marked departures from normal mentality."[17] Up to the end of 1920, some 3,233 insane and feebleminded persons had been sterilized in the United States; no fewer than 2,558 (79 percent) of these were Californians—more than two-thirds of them in insane hospitals, less than one-third in homes for the feebleminded. Up to October 1925, a total of 3,598 insane persons—62 percent of them men—had been sterilized in the state. In June 1928, California still led all states in "asexualization"; the total among the insane had risen to 4,650, of whom 60 percent were men.[18]

17. "An Act to Permit Asexualization of Inmates of the State Hospitals and the Home for . . . Feeble-Minded Children, and Convicts in State Prisons," *The Statutes of California and Amendments to the Codes Passed at the Extra Session of the Thirty-Seventh Legislature* (Sacramento, 1909), pp. 1093-1094; "An Act . . . Repealing the 1909 Law," *Statutes of the . . . Fortieth Session of the Legislature* (Sacramento, 1913), pp. 777-778; "An Act to Amend Section One . . . ," *Statutes of the . . . Extra Session of the Forty-First Legislature* (Sacramento, 1917), pp. 571-572.

18. H. H. Laughlin, *Eugenical Sterilization in the United States* (Chicago, 1922), cited in Dr. Aaron J. Rosanoff, *Manual of Psychiatry*, 6th rev. ed. (New York, 1927), p. 438; *Third Biennial Report of the California Department of Institutions* (Sacramento, 1926), p. 93 (hereafter cited as 3 *Cal.*

Eugenicists had been agitating for sterilization of the unfit for many years before the policy was vigorously implemented. What made the policy so attractive to authorities by the second decade of the century was that it could legitimize the discharge of large numbers of patients from overflowing asylums. For as hospital superintendents, charity administrators, and other physicians came increasingly to urge, the only "danger" that most insane persons presented to the outside community was that they might "leave behind them . . . progeny to carry on the tainted and unhappy stream of heredity." Moreover, sterilization would eventually reduce new admissions too, since the present overcrowding had resulted from "our past custom of permitting defectives to reproduce without restriction."[19] A simple vasectomy in the case of men, and a slightly more difficult salpingectomy (also known as a tubectomy) in the case of women, could eliminate both the threat to the community and the overcrowding of the asylums.

Psychiatric theorists had long argued that heredity was a prime etiological factor in mental disease and other afflictions. Yet most had been careful to add that heredity operated at most as a "predisposing" cause; environmental factors were present in each case as "exciting" causes. Furthermore, until the second decade of the twentieth century, "heredity" commonly referred not to "genetic" transmission, but to the inheritance of both innate and acquired characteristics; an individual would pass on to his or her children both original and "learned" traits. "Heredity" connoted in fact much of what we would designate today as "family environment"; the "heredity"

Dept. Instits. 1926); 4 *Cal Dept. Instits.* 1928, p. 90. For an overview of the California program from the standpoint of two energetic advocates, see E. S. Gosney and Paul Popenoe, *Sterilization for Human Betterment* (New York, 1929).

19. 9 *St. Bd. Char. and Corr.* 1922, p. 34; 8 *St. Bd. Char. and Corr.* 1918, p. 64.

of a child tended to include the behavioral characteristics presently cultivated in his home. A focus on heredity was therefore compatible with a reformist commitment to the rooting out of the environmental sources of an undesirable inheritance—chiefly alcohol, syphilis, and drugs.[20]

But after 1910 a "Mendelian" understanding of heredity—which eliminated the role of the environment by focusing on germ plasm—began to displace the older neo-Lamarckian viewpoint. Now heredity was much more frequently cited as "the most prominent cause of insanity." Hospital superintendents and state officials began to insist that "the offspring of insane persons are almost sure to be weak in some regard. Most frequently they are feebleminded, epileptic, or otherwise pathological. Thus they are an easy prey to every disease of mind and body. This being true, preventing the insane from becoming parents is society's duty. For those with the inheritance and the future to which children of the insane are liable, it is better not to be born." In fact, the insane were a threat not only to their own children, but to the entire race, which shared a single pool of genes. "The whole stream of human life is being constantly polluted by the admixture of the tainted blood of the extremely defective."[21]

California officials further justified their practice by claiming disingenuously that while other states adopted sterilization for "purely eugenic" purposes, California alone did so "for the physical, mental, or moral benefit" of the patient. Interestingly, those benefited by asexuali-

20. Charles E. Rosenberg, "The Bitter Fruit: Heredity, Disease, and Social Thought in Nineteenth Century America," *Perspectives in American History* 8 (1974), 189-235. For examples of the reformist effort to offset undesirable heredity by struggling against the acquired, or environmental, component of that heredity, see "Discussion," 3 *Cal. St. Conf. Char. and Corr.* 1904, pp. 67-68, and 7 *St. Comm. Lun.* 1910, p. 21.

21. 10 *St. Comm. Lun.* 1916, p. 13; 7 *St. Bd. Char. and Corr.* 1916, p. 39; 8 *St. Bd. Char. and Corr.* 1918, p. 62.

zation were not only those inmates with "a definite history of hereditary taint," but also those whose mental abnormality consisted solely in the fact that they "already have more children than they can properly care for." State authorities even "regretted that we cannot reach out further [and] sterilize those defectives who do not come into state institutions, it being estimated that there are perhaps 16,000 defectives in California alone who are being cared for outside of state institutions." In 1911 the superintendent of the Stockton State Hospital proposed making sterilization a condition for obtaining a marriage license for those in the general population with "a taint of insanity in his or her family"—a proposal that was, he admitted, "a little radical," but to which "there would soon be very little objection" when "the probabilities of having an insane or idiotic child were explained."[22]

Sterilization might "possibly prevent the development of a future genius once in a while," the General Superintendent of State Hospitals granted, "but so many who are defective or psychopathic come into the world for lack of sterilization that it is hardly profitable to discuss the question." The superintendents at Stockton and Norwalk agreed that the question was not to be discussed: they sterilized *every* patient below the age of "45 or 50" who was to be discharged. By the time of the First World War, according to state authorities, sterilization had become "the most important part of California's program for the insane." By destroying the reproductive capacities of the insane California was leading the world in . . . prevent[ing] the filling of her institutions in the future."[23]

22. 8 *St. Comm. Lun.* 1912, pp. 19-20; 3 *Cal. Dept. Instits.* 1926, pp. 95, 97; Dr. Fred P. Clark, "What the State Is Doing to Cure Insanity," 6 *Cal. St. Conf. Char. and Corr.* 1911, p. 115.

23. 9 *St. Comm. Lun.* 1914, p. 14; 8 *St. Bd. Char. and Corr.* 1918, p. 63; 2 *Cal. Dept. Instits.* 1924, p. 89; 7 *St. Bd. Char. and Corr.* 1916, p. 39; 10 *St. Comm. Lun.* 1916, p. 53. The superintendents of the Mendocino and Agnews (San Jose) State hospitals had failed by 1918 to lend much enthusi-

In the late nineteenth century, when insanity was considered a product of "civilization"—of the unsettling encounter between an individual and an unstable environment—the appropriate response was to institutionalize and possibly cure those who had succumbed. Rural asylums could harbor them at a safe distance from the disturbing influences of civilized life—particularly alcohol, broken families, the frantic pace of work, and sudden reverses of fortune. Put inversely, but with equal validity, when social policy supported the sequestration of insane persons in asylums far from their families, the appropriate ideology was one that attributed insanity to familial relationships and urban pressures. Policy-makers promoted not only a viewpoint on insanity that may have been common in the society at large, but a viewpoint that served their institutional purposes as well. They in turn helped spread the ideology beyond the institution, grounding it in all likelihood more firmly in the public mind.

In the early twentieth century new institutional demands and a correspondingly new approach to causation emerged simultaneously. It had become clear that insane hospitals not only were incapable of performing cures but also could not accommodate the large numbers of committed individuals. From the standpoint of state policy-makers, a new viewpoint on the cause of mental disorder had become indispensable. The emerging notion that insanity was caused not by civilization, or by present family relationships, but by genetic transmis-

---

asm to the sterilization crusade. For their reticence the State Board of Charities and Corrections upbraided them caustically in 8 *St. Bd. Char. and Corr.* 1918, p. 63. As for the insane themselves, "at first the patients made some objection to the operation, but now they think nothing of it." Dr. Fred P. Clark, Medical Superintendent, Stockton State Hospital, 9 *St. Comm. Lun.* 1914, p. 46. On the sterilization policy in another "progressive" state, see Rudolph Vecoli, "Sterilization: A Progressive Measure?," *Wisconsin Magazine of History* 43 (Spring 1960), 190-202.

sion, served that function admirably. Although the new viewpoint arose independently—it was not invented by hospital physicians or administrators—the fact that it served institutional purposes made it all the more powerful as a social ideology.

The irony of the hereditarian ideology was that even while it legitimized the discharge of sterilized patients—who allegedly no longer posed a threat to the community—it may also have promoted the commitment of a growing proportion of deviants, precisely in order that they too might be rendered "harmless." The skyrocketing rate of hospital admissions after 1912 may therefore have been both a cause and an effect of the spread of the hereditarian ideology. The high rate of admissions led state officials to publicize the hereditary roots of insanity; growing public concern over the "threat to the race" from bad heredity may have led relatives, neighbors, or doctors to petition for the commitment of an ever-growing number of individuals. Although it is impossible to know exactly what the "public" thought, it is clear that, in Mark Haller's phrase, "the myth of the menace of the feebleminded" was especially prevalent in published literature of the second decade of the twentieth century. The California State Board of Charities and Corrections itself asserted in 1916 that "a nation-wide awakening to the menace of the feebleminded" was "one of the most noteworthy movements of public thought."[24]

In the strictest sense the "feebleminded" were distinct from the "insane," but in both popular and professional usage there was considerable overlapping between the

24. Mark H. Haller, *Eugenics: Hereditarian Attitudes in American Thought* (New Brunswick, N.J., 1963), especially Chapter Seven; 7 *St. Bd. Char. and Corr.* 1916, p. 29. See also Peter Tyor, "Segregation or Surgery: The Mentally Retarded in America, 1850-1920," (unpublished Ph.D. dissertation, Northwestern University, 1972), p. 214; Walter I. Trattner, *From Poor Law to Welfare State: A History of Social Welfare in America* (New York, 1974), pp. 168-170; and Roy Lubove, *The Professional Altruist: The Emergence of Social Work as a Career, 1880-1930* (New York, 1969), pp. 66-72.

two. The feebleminded were technically those whose intelligence, as measured by newly designed psychological tests, was "subnormal." But "not infrequently," as one authority noted, "among the feebleminded there is intercurrent insanity; again among the insane there are cases [of] mental defect. It is a distinction in difference, not in kind." In reports of state officials, similarly, the two groups were not clearly distinguished. If the insane patients of the state hospitals had been tested, there is little doubt that a substantial proportion would have been "subnormal." While "75 percent of the inmates, male and female, of jails, reformatories, and penitentiaries" were "imbeciles"—the "middle" grade of feeblemindedness located one rung above the "idiots"—many if not most of the insane would have qualified for the somewhat higher status of the "moron," one who could not "compete on equal terms with his normal fellows or manage himself and his affairs with ordinary prudence." State officials quite consciously advocated this "social definition" of feeblemindedness in preference to the view that limited the concept to idiocy and imbecility. The newer view gave due weight, in their opinion, to the previously neglected "higher grade defectives, the subnormally dull, and those with specialized defects, [who] are responsible for much drunkenness, much prostitution, much crime, and much that tends to disturb public welfare." The social definition of feeblemindedness made it virtually indistinguishable from insanity; both were labels for irrational or imprudent behavior. Institutionalized deviants thus appear by the second decade of the twentieth century to have formed to some degree a common pool of mental defectives, both in the public view and in the view of state charity administrators and psychologists who produced detailed surveys of "mental deviation" under state contracts.[25]

25. Martin W. Barr, *Mental Defectives: Their History, Training, and Treatment* (Philadelphia, 1904), p. 231; 6 *St. Bd. Char. and Corr.* 1915, p. 32; 9 *St. Comm. Lun.* 1914, pp. 14-18; State Legislature, Joint Committee on

Table 1

PERCENT INCREASE IN COMMITMENTS FOR INSANITY, POPULATION,
AND ADULT POPULATION IN SAN FRANCISCO, 1870-1920

Decade	Increase in commitments	Increase in population	Increase in adult population (20 yrs. and over)
1870-1880	30.5	56.5	n.a.
1880-1890	24.9	27.8	n.a.
1890-1900	10.0	14.6	17.4
1900-1910	21.2	21.6	29.8
1910-1920	48.3	21.5	23.1

The figures on commitments for insanity frcm San Francisco between 1870 and 1920 indicate that commitments rose tremendously in the very years that the myth of the "menace of the feebleminded" was most widespread. Of course, the annual number of San Franciscans committed between 1870 and 1920 would be expected to increase, because the population of the city grcw by more than 20 percent in every decade except the 1890s, when the increase was 15 percent. But the increase in commitments was not proportional to the increase in San Francisco's general population, or, more significantly, to the increase in the city's adult population (Table 1).[26] The

Defectives, *Surveys in Mental Deviation in Prisons, Public Schools and Orphanages in California* (Sacramento, 1918), pp. 18-19; Tyor, "Segregation or Surgery," pp. 133-140, 213-214, and *passim.*

26. The rates of increase for the general population and the adult population were calculated from decennial figures in the *Population* volumes of the U.S. Census. To obtain a reliable count for insane commitments in the same years, I averaged the annual figures for a nine-year period. For example, to obtain the number of commitments for "1890," I took the average of the commitments for 1886-1894. This method eliminates the possible error resulting from a single exceptionally high or low annual figure.

Table 2

ANNUAL NUMBER OF COMMITMENTS FOR INSANITY IN
SAN FRANCISCO, 1900-1929

1900: 362	1910: 451	1920: 556
1901: 353	1911: 447	1921: 607
1902: 367	1912: 504	1922: 561
1903: 370	1913: 523	1923: 587
1904: 470	1914: 634	1924: 549
1905: n.a.	1915: 628	1925: 561
1906: 420	1916: 586	1926: 569
1907: 351	1917: 611	1927: 614
1908: 391	1918: 627	1928: 534
1909: 442	1919: 562	1929: 571

population growth rate clearly cannot account for the sharp rise in commitments after 1910. One might suspect that the increase was related to the World War, but the sharp jump actually began in 1912 at the latest.

The number of San Franciscans committed annually between 1912 and the end of the decade was markedly higher than in the earlier period, and the number committed thereafter was actually modestly lower (Table 2). The essentially unchanging annual total of the 1920s is particularly striking because the population of the city was 25 percent greater in 1930 than it had been in 1920. Moreover, the proportion of individuals accused of insanity and ultimately committed by the San Francisco judges also reached a new peak after 1913; the ratio of commitments to court-ordered examinations, which had averaged 68 percent over the two preceding decades, surpassed 80 percent in 1914 and maintained that level through the 1920s.

It is possible, though not demonstrable, that the high number of commitments, and the high ratio of commitments to examinations, between 1912 and 1920 was the result of heightened concern on the part of medical examiners, urban officials, and perhaps the public itself over the threat to the purity of the race. The sterilization campaign, adopted as state policy in an attempt to legitimize a larger number of discharges and relieve overcrowding, may simultaneously have helped to promote a higher number of commitments to the same overburdened hospitals. The hereditarian ideology that justified the campaign may in the end have contributed to its failure.

But state authorities in the early twentieth century did not rely solely on the sterilization crusade. They also hoped to reduce the state hospital population by establishing urban psychopathic wards, a development with major implications for the court commitment process itself. For in creating such wards doctors were seeking not only to provide local treatment facilities for those with "acute" disturbances—disorders thought to be in their "early" stages—but to establish their own professional control over the commitment system, a system subject, in their view, to intolerable obstruction from laymen.

3

From "Railroading" to "Therapy":
The Growth of Medical Control
over Commitment in California,
1870-1930

In the late nineteenth and early twentieth centuries, it is clear, California had a higher proportion of insane residents than other states. We cannot totally rule out the possibility that Californians were more liable to be unbalanced than other Americans. But it seems more likely that the disproportion is explained by the zeal with which California state officials sought to locate, detain, and treat not only those considered "mentally ill," but also a wide variety of other deviants—including, as state hospital physicians put it, "drunkards, simpletons, fools," and "the aged, the vagabond, the helpless." The last chapter examined the broad institutional and ideological developments at the state level; those developments provide the basis for grasping the social and cultural meaning of insanity in California. Here the focus shifts to the commitment process itself, the concrete legal mechanism through which thousands of Californians were sent, for indefinite terms of "treatment," to state hospitals for the insane.

This chapter will deal with the fundamental structure of the commitment mechanism as it developed over a sixty-year period, with special attention to the largely successful struggle by the medical profession to establish its own control of the process. The following three chapters will look in detail at the insane themselves— specifically, the more than 12,000 persons committed between 1906 and 1929 by the Superior Court of San Francisco, the city that accounted for one-fourth to one-third of all California commitments in each year of the late nineteenth and early twentieth centuries.

Prior to the 1850s, commitment procedures in the United States were informal in the extreme. Disturbed individuals could be incarcerated in jails, poorhouses, or asylums by almost anyone—relatives, acquaintances, judges, police, doctors, overseers of the poor. An allegedly insane individual could appeal to no established legal safeguards designed to protect his personal liberty. By the 1850s most states were effectively reducing the number of insane in penal institutions, and were requiring a medical judgment attesting to the individual's insanity. But legal safeguards were still nonexistent.

In the 1860s and 1870s, however, popular anxiety over the perceived threat of "railroading" apparently provoked many state legislatures to re-examine the commitment process. The highly publicized agitation of Mrs. E. P. W. Packard, who claimed in two books and several nationwide tours that her husband had "railroaded" her into the Illinois State Hospital, led directly to laws in several states requiring jury trials in civil commitment proceedings. The phenomenal success of Charles Reade's 1864 novel *Hard Cash*—the story of a sane man's commitment engineered by malevolent business associates— also helped fuel the reform movement.

Medical spokesmen were predictably quick to condemn the new laws. Having only recently obtained laws requiring medical examinations of all allegedly insane persons, doctors now found their informal authority over commitment proceedings seriously challenged. For the rest of the century the medical profession attempted to reverse legislation that, in its view, interfered with the expeditious treatment of the mentally disturbed by trained experts.[1]

In California, where by 1853 the insane were by law committed only to state hospitals and only on the recommendation of at least two "respectable physicians," doctors nevertheless lamented the fact that they did not exercise complete formal control over the commitment process. By the 1870s and 1880s, like their counterparts in other states, they expressed outrage that they were forced to share their authority to bestow the official "insane" label with such nonspecialists as judges and, in some cases, juries. The medical professionals' effort to eliminate "laymen" from the decision-making process was based on their increasingly firm belief that involuntary commitment was not a deprivation of liberty—as lay critics alleged—but a means of treating diseased individuals who were usually ignorant of their own afflictions.[2]

In the closing decades of the nineteenth century an occasional California physician or state hospital official might still warn that the commitment system posed a threat to individual liberties, that the "railroading" of

1. Albert Deutsch, *The Mentally Ill in America* (New York, 1937), pp. 422-426; Gerald N. Grob, *Mental Institutions in America* (New York, 1973), pp. 263-265; Mrs. E. P. W. Packard, *The Prisoner's Hidden Life, or Insane Asylums Unveiled* (Chicago, 1868); Charles Reade, *Hard Cash* (New York, 1864); Barbara Sicherman, "The Quest for Mental Health in America, 1880-1917" (unpublished Ph.D. dissertation, Columbia, 1967), pp. 59-72; A. E. Macdonald, "The Practical Working of the New Lunacy Statutes," *Psychological and Medico-Legal Journal* 2 (March 1875), 146-153.

2. "An Act to Establish an Asylum for the Insane of the State of California," *The Statutes of California Passed at the Fourth Session of the Legislature* (San Francisco, 1853), p. 206. It is possible to detect in the drive for professional control of civil commitment a parallel to the later drive by urban management "experts" to control city government. In both cases an effort was made to remove authority from politically responsible—and hence from the professional standpoint "corruptible"—officials. See Samuel P. Hays, "The Politics of Reform in Municipal Government in the Progressive Era," *Pacific Northwest Quarterly* 55 (October 1964), 157-169.

sane persons into state asylums was an ever-present danger. But by the early twentieth century such expressions of caution were no longer to be found in medical journals or state hospital reports. It was now taken for granted that forced treatment, when ordered and supervised by a professional specialist, was by its very nature therapeutic. The spread of this professional ideology, and the emergence of its institutional counterpart, the urban psychopathic ward—in which doctors could for the first time confine patients without a court hearing—provided the foundation for medical control of commitment in the twentieth century.[3]

II

The movement to establish urban psychopathic treatment centers succeeded in the early twentieth century because it was able to unite two significant and previously antagonistic bodies of nineteenth-century opinion: that of the state hospital superintendents, who felt that county judges were burdening their institutions with too many patients; and that of various "public interest" groups opposed to the "putting away" of innocent victims in those same asylums. In the early twentieth century the hospital superintendents and other state officials came to support the psychopathic ward as a means of depopulating rural asylums and reducing skyrocketing state expenditures for the insane; "public interest" groups backed the innovation as a means of eliminating the stigma of formal commitment to distant

---

3. An interesting indication of the shift in the ideological atmosphere surrounding commitment is the fact that as late as 1884 it was possible for a San Francisco newspaper to publish the names, ages, birthplaces, and occupations of all those sent to state hospitals from the city during the previous year. Such a list would have been unthinkable by the early years of the twentieth century—when it would no longer have been perceived as a legal matter, but as a medical affair. "The Insane for a Year," *San Francisco Morning Call*, January 1, 1884, p. 5.

asylums, and the danger that a sane individual might unjustly be put away for life. Urban physicians and social workers lent additional support, seeing in the psychopathic ward an opportunity to establish more sophisticated standards of treatment, to reach the mentally ill when their disease was in its "acute"—and hence "curable"—stage, and to provide a handy laboratory for the education of professional students.

Throughout the second half of the nineteenth century the medical superintendents of the state hospitals bemoaned what they correctly perceived as the custodial function of their institutions. Regarding themselves, and wishing to be viewed, as specialists in the treatment of persons with disabling mental conditions, they expressed disgust at the role which state law, as utilized by county judges, forced them to play: that of managing detention centers for large numbers of "patients" with no such affliction. "That there are many persons unjustly pronounced to be insane . . . and subsequently committed by the courts," declared the medical superintendent of Agnews State Hospital in 1900, "does not admit of question; and just so long as no vigorous measures are taken to prevent such a course of action, the hospitals of the State will continue to be the receptacle for all forms of human wreckage, regardless of law and justice. It is this excess of population, improperly committed and (strictly speaking) illegally detained, which fills to overflowing the wards of these institutions, interfering sadly with their legitimate work and mission."[4]

County judges and medical examiners, in the superintendents' view, were using the state hospitals as con-

4. Dr. J. A. Crane, "Report of the Medical Superintendent," 2 *St. Comm. Lun.* 1901, p. 60. It was no doubt in the self-interest of the superintendents to attribute the low rate of cures by their institutions to the presence of deviants who were not suited to hospital treatment. Yet their use of those deviants to justify poor recovery rates does not call into question the fact of their dominant presence.

venient depositories for "incompetents" and deviants of all varieties, including some who clearly belonged in the category of the "sane." "In almost every community are persons to be found," noted the Stockton Hospital superintendent in 1892, "who are odd, eccentric, or more or less annoying to their neighbors, but beyond this quite harmless. The temptation is strong, and the effort easy under our present system, to land such people in the asylums."[5] Since the state paid the entire cost of maintaining indefinitely those without funds, county officials had little incentive to provide adequate facilities for detention or care.

The practice was standard in California from the beginning. The Stockton superintendent stated in 1886 that his institution—founded in 1851—had "from an early day carried along on its reports a large contingent, drawn from all quarters, of chronic incurable dements, of imbeciles, dotards, idiots, drunkards, simpletons, fools; a class, in fact, of harmless defectives, usually found in poorhouses elsewhere." As early as 1862 the resident physician of the Stockton Asylum lamented that "the Committing Courts must have lost sight of the nature and purposes of the Institution, and concluded to add to its uses the purposes of a State Poor House. . . . The law requires that a person, to be entitled to the benefits of the Asylum, must be *insane*, and, by reason of insanity, *unsafe to be at large*; yet, notwithstanding this plain provision, we frequently receive [patients] . . . who, if affected in their minds at all, it is [*sic*] the weakness of old age, or intemperance, or perhaps most commonly both together."[6]

5. Dr. H. N. Rucker, "Report of the Medical Superintendent," *Thirty-Ninth and Fortieth Reports of the Stockton State Insane Asylum* (Sacramento, 1892), p. 29.

6. Dr. W. H. Mays, "Report of the Medical Superintendent," *Thirty-Third and Thirty-Fourth Annual Reports of the Insane Asylum of the State of California at Stockton* (Sacramento, 1886), pp. 15-16; Dr. W. P. Tilden,

The state legislature was sufficiently concerned by 1872 to pass a statute barring the commitment of cases of "harmless, chronic mental unsoundness or acute mania *a potu.*" But the measure—reiterated in the 1885 Act to Prevent the Overcrowding of Asylums—"has been practically inoperative," remarked Stockton's superintendent H. N. Rucker in 1892, and it remained a dead letter into the twentieth century. "From the 1850s to the present," one hospital physician stated in 1908, "every pauper who was mentally weak from old age or any other cause would be picked up by the county officials and sent to the state asylum for the county's own protection"—"protection," clearly, not against dangerous behavior, but against expense, and in many cases, as Chapter Six will show, against conduct that implicitly or explicitly challenged hallowed middle-class norms.[7]

Why then did the superintendents not discharge those patients who in their view were illegally committed? Like the county medical examiners and judges, they doubtless felt obliged to protect themselves against adverse public reaction to the discharging of large numbers of persons officially labeled "unsafe to be at large." In Dr. Rucker's words, "Although apparently not dangerous to be at large, the asylum physicians are loath to discharge such cases when the commitment is seemingly made

---

"Report of the Resident Physician," *Tenth Annual Report of the Trustees of the Insane Asylum* (Sacramento, 1863), pp. 21, 32-33. Italics in the original.

7. California State Legislature, Statutes of California Passed at the *Nineteenth Session of the Legislature* (Sacramento, 1872), p. 678; California State Legislature, *Statutes of California Passed at the Twenty-Sixth Session of the Legislature* (Sacramento, 1885), p. 37; Rucker, "Report of the Medical Superintendent," p. 29; Dr. John W. Robertson, "Discussion," 5 *Cal. St. Conf. Char. and Corr.* 1909, p. 48. "Mania *a potu,*" literally "madness from drink," is in psychiatric parlance a state of extreme excitement produced by alcohol. Leland E. Hinsie and Robert Jean Campbell, *Psychiatric Dictionary*, 4th ed. (New York, 1970), p. 446.

necessary by the statement or affidavit of someone that the patient has threatened life and property."[8]

Moreover, the superintendents were convinced that most of the harmless patients who filled their dormitories had nowhere to go, and that they received much better care at the state hospital than they could hope to obtain in county almshouses or hospitals. Though these "defectives" were not insane, the insane hospital constituted the best available shelter. "No doubt," remarked Superintendent F. W. Hatch of Agnews State Hospital in 1893, "there are persons in our asylums who are not, strictly speaking, dangerous to life or property; but they are not competent to be at large for all that. Every sentiment of charity and every impulse of reason urge that until they can be cared for elsewhere, they cannot be turned adrift."[9]

Proposals for a state almshouse, which might have eliminated both inadequate county care and commitment of the "non-insane" to state hospitals, got nowhere— though they were urged by superintendents throughout the nineteenth and early twentieth centuries. Without such an almshouse, wrote the Napa Hospital superintendent in 1877, the hospitals would remain "terribly overcrowded" with persons "excluded by law from admission into the Asylums of this State, but who are nevertheless committed by the Judges . . . for the reason that there is no other place to send them. The law of the land is violated . . . at the earnest and irresistible demands of the law of humanity." Because of their persistence in placing harmless individuals in insane asylums, he added indignantly, "Californians [are] spoken of as the craziest people in the world."[10]

8. Rucker, "Report of the Medical Superintendent," p. 29.

9. Dr. F. W. Hatch, cited in "Commitment of the Insane," *San Francisco Examiner*, October 3, 1893, p. 10.

10. Dr. E. T. Wilkins, "Resident Physician's Report," *Report of the Board of Trustees of the Napa State Hospital for the Insane* (Sacramento, 1877), pp. 21-22.

In most instances the superintendents deplored the fact that their hospitals in fact functioned as "receptacles" for "all forms of human wreckage." But some hospital physicians took the view that stretching the intent of the commitment law was an enlightened practice. In 1903 Dr. John W. Robertson, formerly of the Napa State Hospital and then superintendent of the renowned Livermore Sanitarium, explained that California had a high rate of insane commitments because "its peculiar method of care makes the asylums popular." The state hospitals met with public favor, he claimed proudly, "because of the great facilities they offer for the disposal of all who are decrepit from age, from mental infirmity, or who, for any other reason, have become burdens on the public at large, or whose friends do not feel equal to their care. Though the law is sufficiently explicit that only the dangerously insane can be committed, the law is constantly evaded." That evasion, according to Dr. Robertson, was justifiable on humanitarian grounds. "California believes that, in place of allowing irresponsible individuals to wander, a care to their friends, a menace to society, or a burden to some particular community . . . all such should be gathered up in her great institutions and at least be humanely cared for. . . . She certainly deserves praise for so nobly shouldering the entire responsibility not only for those mentally disordered, but for the helpless and incompetent who have flocked here in such numbers." The flood-tide of deviants could be contained only by indulging in the convenient fiction that they were insane. California—"the dumping ground for the off-scourings of creation"—had assumed the noble burden of detaining not only the mentally disturbed, but a "heterogeneous collection of the epileptics, the aged, the vagabond, the helpless" and other such "irresponsible individuals."[11]

11. Dr. John W. Robertson, "Prevalence of Insanity in California," *American Journal of Insanity* 60 (July 1903), 77, 86, 81.

Dr. Robertson was more inclined to sanction the mass confinement of burdensome individuals than the majority of superintendents—in part, perhaps, because he was no longer employed in one of the state hospitals, all five of which were egregiously overcrowded. But state hospital officials occasionally expressed the same view. The state's first asylum had undeniably "prosecuted the great Christian charity for which it was established," declared the State Board of Health in 1873, "freely open[ing] its doors to . . . the sick and the cast down, the suicidal and homicidal, the inebriate and the debauchée. . . . More than this, it has relieved many families, relatives, and friends from continual danger, dreadful anxiety, and the necessary constant watching, which would involve the loss of their time and services to the State." This report was the only one to suggest that a liberal commitment policy would actually constitute an economic advantage.[12]

In general, the state's medical superintendents—true to their professional self-image as specialists in the care of mental "illness"—urged a narrow interpretation of the commitment law. Only by limiting admissions to "well-defined mental diseases," in the words of the Mendocino superintendent in 1916, "instead of including, as now, dream states, temporary upsets in defective make-ups, and a certain number of [alcoholic] delirium tremens cases," could therapeutic treatment actually take place. Commitment proceedings, Dr. Hoisholt of the Stockton State Hospital informed an elite audience at San Francisco's Commonwealth Club in 1911, were conducted by "a Superior Court judge who knows nothing at all about mental disease and a few physicians in general practice who know little or nothing about the subject. . . . The commitment of patients who are not insane is not uncommon." Without a change in the commitment procedure, California's state hospitals—all disastrously ex-

12. 2 *Cal. St. Bd. Health* 1873, p. 68.

ceeding capacity, with patients commonly sleeping in corridors—would continue to suffer from conditions which, in the view of one member of the State Board of Charities and Corrections in 1918, "would seem to be enough to drive a normal person insane."[13]

It is important to stress that the asylum physicians' drive to restrict commitments to the "truly insane" was in effect an effort to redefine, to narrow, the exceedingly broad role that California's asylums had, in their view, always played. But from the beginning, other state and county legislators and officials had pursued a liberal commitment policy. Abolishing a procedure that allowed local communities to unload troubling individuals on the state at no cost to themselves would prove difficult, indeed probably impossible. Even when, in the early twentieth century, medical men assumed virtually complete control over the commitment process, asylums continued to function, in Dr. Robertson's pithy formulation, as "dumping grounds for the off-scourings of creation." For doctors did not constitute a uniform, homogeneous interest group. Although all physicians could agree that "laymen" ought to be excluded from decisions about insanity, many doctors at the local level—particularly the general practitioners appointed by the County Superior Courts to serve as medical examiners—continued to support the removal to state hospitals of troublesome though sane individuals. They followed the by-then traditional practice of declaring many of them "insane," whatever their actual mental condition.

Voices from outside the medical profession—former patients, lawyers, Justices of the State Supreme Court, and leading newspapers claiming to speak in the "public interest"—constituted the second form of opposition to

---

13. Dr. Robert L. Richards, "Report of the Medical Superintendent," 10 *St. Comm. Lun.* 1916, pp. 86-87; Dr. Hoisholt, cited in "Inhuman Treatment of the Insane," *San Francisco Call*, March 12, 1911, p. 30; Dr. John R. Haynes, "Sterilization," 8 *St. Bd. Char. and Corr.* 1918, p. 64.

the commitment procedure in the late nineteenth century. Popular hostility to commitment practices—based on the suspicion that many inmates had been "railroaded" into the asylum—was, as previously noted, widespread throughout the United States after the Civil War. Popular feelings about commitment were apparently still intense in San Francisco as late as 1893, when a furor over railroading erupted in the daily press. According to a state law first enacted in 1864, a warrant was to be issued to every person charged with insanity, and his case was to be heard personally by a judge in the presence of "two or more witnesses having had frequent intercourse with the accused during the time of the alleged insanity."[14] But in practice, warrants were not issued and witnesses were not present at the examination. Two physicians examined accused individuals in a basement room of the City Hall—without revealing the purpose of the examination—and then made a recommendation which the judge rubber-stamped.

The San Francisco County Clerk's reports for the late nineteenth century suggest that the public perception of "railroading" may well have been based on fact. Between 1873—the first year for which figures are available—and 1885, an average of 69 percent of those charged with insanity and examined by court-appointed physicians were committed. Percentages for single years ranged from a low of 60 percent to a high of 76 percent. But beginning in 1886, when the proportion committed reached 79 percent, a major shift occurred. By 1888 the figure was 86 percent, by 1889 an incredible 97 percent. In 1891 and 1892, immediately prior to the public furor detailed in newspaper reports, the proportions sent to the asylums were 93 percent and 91 percent. Of the 368 and 356 persons examined respectively in 1891 and 1892,

14. "An Act amendatory of . . . an Act concerning the Insane Asylum of California," *Statutes of California Passed at the Fifteenth Session of the Legislature* (Sacramento, 1864), p. 325.

only 22 and 20 respectively were *not* committed. The overall average for the years 1886 to 1892 was 86 percent committed.

It is no doubt significant that the years of the sharp rise in the ratio of commitments to examinations were the very years, according to the County Clerk's reports, that witnessed an abrupt decline in commitments to the local Home for Inebriates. Commitments to that institution averaged 28 per year between 1875 and 1886. But between 1887 and 1891, when the Home shut its doors, only two persons per year were committed. Presumably some of the city's inebriates were committed to state hospitals for insanity during those years, as indeed many of them were in the early twentieth-century years covered by the Superior Court records utilized in this study. But even if all of the inebriates previously committed to the Home were sent to the state hospital, they could not account for the entire increase in the percentage of examinations that resulted in commitment. Although the steep rise in the proportion of those commitments after 1885 does not establish that examiners were conspiring to "railroad" people to asylums, it does reveal, at the very least, a growing willingness to recommend the commitment of almost anyone charged with insanity.

When the Reverend Joseph Nouri—committed for claiming he had beheld the Ark of Noah atop Mount Ararat—was finally released from the Napa State Hospital, he made his case public. In response, a group of concerned lawyers formed the California Association for the Protection of Persons Charged with Insanity, which according to the *Morning Call* promised "to work a reform in the summary method, in vogue in this state, of railroading people to insane asylums." Seconding the *Call*, the *Examiner* ran a lengthy two-week series on a situation "as scandalous as anything that ever afflicted the unfortunate hero of *Very Hard Cash*."[15]

15. "Trial by Jury—Against Railroading of Insane People," *San Francisco*

"Who is safe?" wondered the *Examiner*. "The liberty of every human being in the city is at the mercy of two men. It needs only for an enemy to get the ear of Dr. Windell or Dr. Lilienthal [the court-appointed medical examiners] . . . and the job is done." "There is no doubt," declared one of the founding attorneys of the Association, "that Nouri was railroaded to an insane asylum. He may have had an hallucination about the ark on the mountain, but he is sound on every other question and as harmless as a child." The Association, which claimed over one hundred dues-paying members by January 1894, investigated several other cases of alleged railroading and assigned an attorney to supervise every medical examination performed in what the *Examiner* graphically termed "the little den . . . the gloomy room in the basement with its odor of mystery."[16]

As a result of the publicity, a Superior Court judge ordered that all commitment proceedings were to be held in open court, "to the end that public interests and private rights may be best subserved and protected." The open court system "will undoubtedly make a great deal of work, but it will effectually prevent any 'railroading' of sane men into asylums." The *Examiner*, greatly relieved, concluded editorially that "for the present at least, the vicious system of insanity commitments heretofore prevailing in this city has been suddenly and completely

---

Morning Call, August 14, 1894, p. 8; "Insanity Commissioners and the Law," Editorial, *San Francisco Examiner*, September 23, 1893, p. 4. It is especially noteworthy that the editorial writer assumes readers to be familiar with the story of *Hard Cash* (some editions of which were called *Very Hard Cash*), first published thirty years earlier.

16. "Insanity Commissioners and the Law," p. 4; J. B. de las Casas, cited in "Freed from a Madhouse," *San Francisco Examiner*, September 20, 1893, p. 3; C. K. Jenness, *The Charities of San Francisco, A Directory* (San Francisco, 1894), p. 45; "A Star Chamber Abolished," *San Francisco Examiner*, September 22, 1893, p. 3; "Held Without Warrant," *Examiner*, September 24, 1893, p. 4.

reformed. . . . In some cases people as sane as their persecutors were locked up to get them out of the way; in others inebriates, epileptics, and imbeciles were passed off as insane in order to shift their support upon the state. . . . Fortunately the courts in San Francisco seem at last fully awake to the needs of the situation."[17] County Clerk reports reveal that the open court system in fact had the predicted effect. From 1893 to 1895, only 66 percent of those examined were committed. The average for the two decades from 1893 to 1913 was 68 percent.

The prevalence of public suspicion about commitment methods and about the asylums themselves is also clearly revealed in contemporary medical literature and reports. In 1892 the Napa Hospital Trustees warned that any "destitute and friendless" person with "strong eccentricities" was liable to be "hurried away, railroad speed, to an insane asylum." Even those medical observers who denied the fact of railroading granted that the public believed it to be commonplace. In 1894, in the immediate wake of the San Francisco controversy, Dr. W. S. Whitwell, Chairman of the Committee on Diseases of the Mind and Nervous System of the California Medical Society, attacked the "prevalent idea existing in the world today that within the walls of Insane Asylums are many persons who do not belong there. . . . As a fanciful dream stirring the sympathies of the sentimentally inclined, this delusion is a success, but as a matter of fact it is pure fiction." Twelve years later, when the medical superintendents assembled to discuss such issues as their public

17. "A Star Chamber Abolished," p. 3; "Declining Lunacy Rate," Editorial, *San Francisco Examiner*, September 30, 1893, p. 6. Concern over railroading was expressed in news stories well into the twentieth century, although the rhetoric was considerably more subdued. "Says Wife Tried to Place Him in Asylum," *San Francisco Bulletin*, January 4, 1911, p. 11; "Agnews Abuses Charged in Court Battle," *San Francisco Examiner*, May 14, 1919, p. 13; "The Brutality at Agnews Charged," *San Jose Mercury Herald*, June 12, 1919, p. 1.

image, Superintendent Stocking of Agnews State Hospital still had to bemoan the popular attitude. "There is a great feeling that people are often railroaded to hospitals. . . . I have never seen one yet that was railroaded to a hospital. Still, notwithstanding," he concluded ruefully, "that is the public feeling." "The world at large," complained another superintendent in 1908, "believes that insane people are railroaded to insane asylums." As late as 1916 the State Board of Charities and Corrections continued to lament the sad state of public opinion. "The horror with which people look upon treatment in state institutions is amazing." In fact, "in one locality," the Board noted with disgust, "an open and organized effort to discredit the State hospitals" was flourishing.[18]

III

Beginning in 1894 medical professionals at both state and local levels exhibited a new sense of urgency about what they regarded as popular ignorance of the needs of the mentally ill. Open court proceedings—as ordered by the Superior Court judge in San Francisco—were anathema to physicians. Putting the mentally ill on public display, they argued, could only make their afflictions worse; indeed, the trauma of such "quasi-criminal" hearings might render therapy impossible. Even though doctors working with the insane at the state level resented the role of county physicians in "unloading" many sane deviants on the state, both groups were united in urging that commitment proceedings should be controlled by doctors, not judges, and should be private, not open to public scrutiny. "The California law is unjust to the

18. *Biennial Report of the Trustees of . . . the Napa State Hospital for the Insane* (Sacramento, 1892), p. 12; Dr. W. S. Whitwell, "The Commitment of the Insane," *Transactions of the Medical Society of the State of California* 24 (1894) p. 223; 4 *Cal. St. Conf. Char. and Corr.* 1906, p. 153; 5 *Cal. St. Conf. Char. and Corr.* 1909, p. 52; 7 *St. Bd. Char. and Corr.* 1916, p. 46.

insane," declared Dr. Whitwell, "for it leaves the commitment in the hands of the judge and not as it should be entirely at the discretion of the medical profession."[19]

With the victory of the "sentimentally inclined" in San Francisco—a city which in the 1890s provided almost one-third of all state insane commitments—the California Medical Society, the State Board of Health, and the medical superintendents of the state hospitals set out to secure legislation that would put commitment in the hands of doctors. "The interference of non-experts," remarked one former superintendent, "is certain to be dangerous and . . . ought to be discouraged." Since "most persons think of these institutions as places of horror," whereas in fact "in our day the average asylum is really a pleasant hospital," only those who understood their true character could take responsibility for committing persons to them.[20] From the doctors' standpoint, judges— who in practice had given them a virtually free hand from 1853 to 1893—were now the key obstacle to medical control.

The medical campaign came to apparent fruition in 1897, when the state legislature enacted a new Lunacy Law. The new measure, which passed easily by votes of 60-0 in the Assembly and 22-6 in the Senate, did away with open court hearings, and even eliminated the older requirement that a judge personally examine the accused individual. Two physicians could now legally examine any person without disclosing the purpose of the examination, without in fact even revealing that they were doctors or were in the process of examining the person

19. Whitwell, "The Commitment of the Insane," p. 229. See also Dr. James E. Lilienthal, "The Necessity for New Laws Governing the Commitment of the Insane and the Utility of Voluntary Admission to Asylums," *Pacific Coast Journal of Homeopathy* 3 (January 1895), 1-3. Dr. Lilienthal was in 1895 a San Francisco Superior Court medical examiner.

20. Dr. W. H. Mays, cited in "The Commitment of the Insane," *San Francisco Examiner*, October 3, 1893, p. 10.

at all.[21] For as the physicians dealing with the mentally
disturbed had long argued, to apprise such a person of
the nature of the proceedings might well cause him to
resist hospitalization and thereby undermine the treatment of which he was in need. With the passage of the
Lunacy Law doctors believed that they had finally succeeded in protecting the health of sick persons who had
heretofore been hurt by "sentimentalists" overly concerned with a patient's alleged "rights."[22]

But four years later the measure was a dead letter. In
December 1901, the California Supreme Court, by a vote
of 4-1, declared the Lunacy Law unconstitutional. "There
is no provision," the Court ruled, "for giving to the
alleged insane person any notice of the proceedings
against him. . . . The first intimation that he may have
thereof may be when the sheriff takes him into his custody
under the order of commitment." In conclusion, the
Court held—to the bitter consternation of medical professionals—that "an order for the commitment of a
person to an insane hospital is essentially a judgment by
which he is deprived of his liberty."[23]

21. *Journal of the Assembly during the 32nd Session of the Legislature of
the State of California* (Sacramento, 1897), p. 1136; *Journal of the Senate
during the 32nd Session of the Legislature of the State of California*
(Sacramento, 1897), p. 1104. The new Lunacy Law also changed the names
of state institutions from "asylums" to "hospitals" and underscored the role
of the State Commission in Lunacy—created on paper in 1887—in over-
seeing the operations of the hitherto largely independent asylums. This
state agency was partly a rationalizing, centralizing measure in the interests
of efficiency, but it was also a public relations endeavor, an attempt to
reduce popular distrust of asylums by creating a supposed "watchdog"
commission. The same can be said about the establishment in 1903 of the
State Board of Charities and Corrections, except that the Board, unlike the
Commission, did upon occasion play a watchdog role. *Statutes of California
and Amendments to the Codes, Passed at the 32nd Session of the Legislature* (Sacramento, 1897), ch. 227, p. 326.

22. "Discussion," 4 *Cal St. Conf. Char. and Corr.* 1906, pp. 150-154.

23. C. P. Pomeroy, *Reports of Cases Determined in the Supreme Court of
the State of California*, vol. 134 (San Francisco, 1902), pp. 628, 632; "Nulli-
fies State Lunacy Law," *San Francisco Call*, December 4, 1901, p. 14.

The case attracted national attention. It revealed to doctors and other reformers that their efforts to make commitment a medical rather than a legal proceeding were blocked not only by popular ignorance but also by powerful institutions. The official organ of New York's Charity Organization Society, expressing the same outrage as California's medical men, stated indignantly that "the ruling of the court is another evidence of the barbaric conception of insanity which lingers in the minds of jurists. . . . The insane can never receive the kind of care and treatment accorded to other sick persons as long as the laws define them as a class requiring 'commitment' under the same procedure as a criminal receives under trial. . . . The accused one must be convicted (of being sick) before he can receive the healing influences of skilled treatment and curative environment."[24]

The doctors could take some comfort in the fact that the San Francisco judges adopted the practice of holding commitment hearings at the hospital where the alleged insane were detained, rather than in the Superior Court. That shift in location reduced public exposure to a minimum. Yet a hearing was still necessary, and the sick person could not help thinking, physicians warned, that he had been convicted of a crime. In the words of Superintendent Stocking: "It is often difficult to convince a patient, who does not recognize his own confusion of mind, that he has not been tried and committed for some criminal offense. It also necessitates dragging the sick and the feeble through a trying ordeal and landing them

---

24. "The Insane," *Charities* 8 (January 1902), 6. The California superintendents expressed their shock over the decision in their "Discussion," 3 *Cal. St. Conf. Char. and Corr.* 1904, p. 72. Dr. Leonard Stocking of the Agnews State Hospital confessed that "the recent adverse decision of the Supreme Court" had caused "not a little embarrassment to the management" because some hospitalized patients were filing habeus corpus suits in an effort to prove their own commitments had been illegal. 3 *St. Comm. Lun.* 1902, p. 60.

at the hospital exhausted, with their chances of possible restoration lessened."[25]

IV

The Supreme Court decision of 1901 played a major role in galvanizing the organized movement for urban psychopathic wards. The decision of the Court forced California medical professionals to realize that not only popular "ignorance" but also legal traditions and powerful judicial institutions stood in the way of medical control of commitment. In the first decade of the new century, therefore, doctors shifted their strategy. Instead of attempting to reform the commitment procedure, they proposed to bypass the court altogether, hoping that the civil commitment procedure would thereby fall into disuse. Two routes seemed possible: first, voluntary commitments to the state hospitals, and second, voluntary or involuntary commitments to temporary urban treatment centers. Both alternatives were pushed vigorously up to 1911, when the first became legally possible. After that date the organized campaign for the psychopathic ward took on even more crucial significance, because it was soon discovered that very few mentally disturbed persons wished to avail themselves of the opportunity to enter state hospitals by choice.

The theory behind the voluntary admission proposal was simple. Since physicians believed that many afflicted individuals either actively desired hospital treatment or could be persuaded to undergo it—objecting only to the stigma of a court hearing—a simple legislative act could remedy much of the inadequacy of the "quasi-criminal" commitment system. Individuals could make application directly to the medical superintendent of a state hospital. "We have faith to believe," declared the State Board of Charities and Corrections in 1910, "that if such a law

25. Dr. Leonard Stocking, "Report of the Medical Superintendent," 4 *St. Comm. Lun.* 1904, p. 77.

were enacted, it would be but a few years when most cases would come in this way."[26]

That prediction proved wildly optimistic. Between 1911 and 1930 voluntary admissions never amounted in any year to more than 9 percent of the total admissions. Dr. Stocking of Agnews State Hospital, whose institution was entirely rebuilt after the 1906 earthquake and was the most popular among the voluntary patients, might claim in 1914 that "the numerous cases of voluntary commitments" revealed the weakening of "the old feeling that the 'insane asylum' is a place to be greatly dreaded." But even his hospital never had a voluntary admission rate in any single year of more than 12 percent. Moreover, some voluntary patients were discharged and readmitted more than once in a single year, which somewhat inflates the voluntary rate. Curiously, Dr. Stocking believed he could employ the latter fact to buttress his argument that the mental hospital was no longer a place to be dreaded. "Very frequently," he reported, "one of the discharged [voluntary] patients, who is unable to get along on the outside, voluntarily comes back and says he wants to stay." He did not comment on the possibility that such a patient might have been "unable to get along on the outside" precisely because he had been hospitalized. A patient's voluntary return to the hospital, in other words, might constitute evidence of the stigma still associated with such hospitalization—a stigma that prevented the patient, for example, from obtaining a job. Dr. Stocking believed that hospital treatment was at best therapeutic and at worst neutral; in itself it could not be harmful to the patient.[27]

26. "Care of the Insane," 4 *St. Bd. Char. and Corr.* 1910, p. 23.

27. "Agnews State Hospital," 6 *St. Bd. Char. and Corr.* 1915, p. 101. Thomas Scheff, *Being Mentally Ill* (Chicago, 1966), p. 84, points out that medical and psychiatric professionals still typically share Dr. Stocking's assumption that treatment, by definition, cannot be deleterious in itself. On the acceptance by many "mentally ill" persons of their role as sick persons, see Scheff, pp. 84-92.

Other superintendents did not consider the voluntary program to have been so successful. Dr. A. W. Hoisholt of Napa concluded in 1918 that "people do not make much use of it"—not, apparently, because of any suspicion about or hostility to the institution, but "because they do not know of its existence." Whether through ignorance or opposition, only a small percentage of mentally disturbed persons took advantage of the voluntary admission law. Involuntary commitments made up more than 90 percent of all new admissions from 1911 to 1930.[28]

Even before the passage of the law, California's medical professionals had been pushing the second, and ultimately the major, alternative to court-ordered commitment: the erection of a psychopathic ward in the city itself. The failure of the voluntary admission program only intensified the already vigorous campaign to create urban treatment centers.

The idea of erecting such centers was not in itself a product of the first years of the twentieth century. As early as 1872 Dr. A. B. Stout of San Francisco, addressing the California Medical Society's annual convention, urged the establishment of what he called "probationary asylums for the insane in large cities." While granting that "the propriety of locating asylums . . . in situations remote and secluded from the excitement of cities, re-

---

28. Dr. A. W. Hoisholt, "Report of the Medical Superintendent," 11 *St. Comm. Lun.* 1918, p. 58. Two useful articles that place the California voluntary admission program in national perspective are George S. Adams, "Voluntary Patients in an Insane Hospital," *Proceedings*, National Conference of Charities and Corrections, 1907 (Indianapolis, n.d.), pp. 434-437; and Winfred Overholser, "The Voluntary Admission Law: Certain Legal and Psychiatric Aspects," *American Journal of Psychiatry* 3 (January 1924), 475-490. Twenty-seven other states had voluntary admission procedures in 1924. But only 6 states had voluntary rates over 10 percent, and only Michigan, the first state to establish a university-based psychopathic hospital (at Ann Arbor in 1906), surpassed 16 percent. It had a voluntary rate of 22 percent. Overholser, p. 477.

freshed with the pure air of the country. . . cannot be contested," he pointed out that many patients were unnecessarily and unjustly committed. "Many a sane person has, on [false] imputations, been confined, as it were, incarcerated, to his great damage, for long periods in an asylum." Since "it is oftentimes impossible to arrive at a true decision in doubtful cases," there was a clear need for a probationary facility, where an individual's real mental status could be ascertained over a period of days or, if necessary, weeks. Moreover, in "the frequent cases of delirium tremens, cerebral alcoholism without delirium tremens, of mania, of less acute insanity from menstrual disturbance, uterine disease," or other "transitory" forms of "mental alienation," treatment and recovery could occur in the city asylum, thus protecting "the record of families from the taint of hereditary insanity" while at the same time helping to reduce costs at the state level.[29]

Dr. Stout's plea apparently fell on deaf ears, for it was not echoed by other medical men or legislators in the years that followed. His address displayed such overriding concern for the rights of those detained that doctors connected with the state treatment of the insane must have been thoroughly displeased with his message. Furthermore, since he himself accepted the standard nineteenth-century view that "landscape scenery to divert the mind from its distracting griefs" was an incontestable advantage, it should not be surprising if most physicians preferred to continue erecting rural asylums rather than to build one in San Francisco. Shortly before Dr. Stout spoke, in fact, construction of the state's second asylum had been approved. Only when, at the start of the twentieth century, it became evident that the legislature would fund no more asylums, and that the five existing institutions were hopelessly overburdened, were doctors at the

29. Dr. A. B. Stout, "Report on Probationary Asylums for the Insane in Large Cities," 2 *Cal. St. Bd. Health* 1873, pp. 97-99, 102.

state level ready to turn as a group to the idea of urban treatment facilities.[30]

Thirty years after Dr. Stout's address, the State Commission in Lunacy brought state policy into line with his proposal. In 1902 the Commission urged that "a few small hospitals for the treatment of acute recent cases only, [be] located in some of our largest cities, like San Francisco, Oakland, and Los Angeles." The Commission, led by Dr. F. W. Hatch, General Superintendent of the State Hospitals, stated quite precisely the cardinal advantage of such a system. "Patients should be admitted to them on the certificate of two physicians," Dr. Hatch argued, "and *legal committal could wait* on the progress of the case." "It may be," he added, "that public opinion is not ready for this innovation, but that it would work a great benefit . . . cannot be questioned."[31]

Dr. Hatch's address at the biennial convention of the State Conference of Charities and Corrections in February 1904 marked the opening salvo in an organized campaign to turn public opinion around. "Modern treatment of the insane," as Dr. Hatch titled his address, meant early treatment; insanity, like other diseases, could be cured much more frequently if medical intervention occurred at the first sign of disturbance. Yet the legal impediment to early treatment at state hospitals ap-

30. Stout, "Report on Probationary Asylums," p. 97. It is important to note that as early as the middle of the nineteenth century eastern cities erected "municipal asylums" for the detention of troublesome persons— who were usually both poor and foreign-born. Yet these institutions were by intention custodial; since state facilities were either inadequate or too far away, city authorities decided to detain disturbing citizens locally. Proponents of psychopathic hospitals in the early twentieth century believed, like Dr. Stout, that such hospitals would offer distinctly therapeutic care for "early" cases of mental disorder and that treatment would in all cases be temporary. Hence the early municipal asylums were in no sense prototypes for the later urban treatment centers. On the municipal asylums, see Grob, *Mental Institutions in America*, pp. 212-214.

31. 3 *St. Comm. Lun.* 1902, p. 10. Italics added.

peared insurmountable. The only solution was "a separate building for the acute insane in connection with a general hospital . . . under municipal control." In the city itself "the best minds in the profession may be obtained," and patients could be treated and released without "having attached to them, after recovery, the possible blot of having been committed to an insane asylum." Dr. Hatch again granted that the idea "cannot be put into practice at once," but now added that "public opinion will have to be molded into shape." Such a measure constituted the only conceivable way in which the mentally disturbed could obtain the early treatment physicians believed they required—and the only way in which doctors could secure their long-sought control over the treatment of the mentally ill.[32]

In discussion following Dr. Hatch's address, Dr. Hoisholt of the Stockton asylum voiced the view that a separate hospital for the acute insane at some remove from the city was more desirable than an additional facility at the San Francisco County Hospital. Such, he argued, was the enlightened practice in the most advanced countries; he was "sorry to say that the State of California was not up with Germany and the northern part of Europe."[33] Yet "it is true," Dr. Hoisholt felt compelled to add, "that an additional asylum for the acute insane . . . would perhaps not take well with the public. The public has an

32. Dr. F. W. Hatch, "Modern Treatment of the Insane," 3 *Cal. St. Conf. Char. and Corr.* 1904, pp. 61, 64.

33. Dr. A. W. Hoisholt, "Discussion," 3 *Cal. St. Conf. Char. and Corr.* 1904, p. 66. Psychiatric reformers, like other progressives, appealed to the example of enlightened nations (and in the case of California to the example of enlightened eastern states) in an effort to establish the demonstrable need for reform. If America, or California, were to be "modern" it would have to emulate the most advanced practices in the world. The model that reformers invoked most commonly prior to World War I was Germany. See, for example, L. Pierce Clark and H. P. Alan Montgomery, "Suggestions and Plans for Psychopathic Wards, Pavilions, and Hospitals for American Cities," *American Journal of Insanity* 61 (July 1904), 1-10.

idea that they have too many insane asylums now." He
would therefore support Dr. Hatch's plan since it stood a
better chance of obtaining the public's approval. Since no
stigma was attached, it appeared, to treatment in a general hospital, it would be possible to add treatment for
mental illness to its functions without encountering the
same public hostility that insane asylums continued to
experience.[34]

Neither Dr. Hatch nor Dr. Hoisholt publicly considered the question of how to treat individuals who did
not desire such medical attention. But it was evident,
even if unstated, that involuntary treatment would figure
prominently in the operations of the psychopathic ward,
because it was to detain for observation and diagnosis
individuals officially charged with insanity. Since involuntary confinement would by law be temporary, however, it would presumably not carry the same stigma—or
meet the same legal checks—as formal, indefinite commitment. If a patient proved incurable by the most advanced methods available in the city, then court-ordered
commitment to a state hospital could still be invoked as a
last resort. It is not surprising, however, that physicians
seeking public and professional support for a major
institutional innovation did not publicize what many
laymen would certainly have considered its least attractive function.

The medical superintendents of the state hospitals, as
would be expected, lent their vigorous support to the
proposal, since it seemed sure to alleviate the overcrowding they had been complaining about for decades.
The concurrent proposal for voluntary admissions to the
state hospitals did not possess that signal advantage.
Pointing out that 40 percent of his admissions came
from San Francisco, Napa Superintendent Elmer Stone

34. Hoisholt, "Discussion," 3 *Cal. St. Conf. Char. and Corr.* 1904, pp.
66-67.

argued in 1909 that "a psychopathic ward in the city of San Francisco will result in relieving our state institutions from the care of many cases that would recover within a few weeks' time under proper care and treatment."[35] Such a ward, that is, would provide better care than his own hospital and would therefore in the long run reduce his patient population.

The psychopathic ward would also provide a place of temporary detention and observation for those deviants who, though evidently not insane, had been customarily committed to state hospitals since the 1850s—to the displeasure of many superintendents. "We are vitally interested in the proposed San Francisco psychopathic hospital," declared Mendocino Superintendent Robert Richards, who received two-thirds of his patients from San Francisco, "so that commitment may be restricted to well-defined mental diseases." "The state," concluded Dr. Hatch in a 1914 report, "has many burdens on its hands, and the counties should come forward and help in this advanced work."[36]

V

Gradually the counties did come forward. In San Francisco a loose alliance of elite reformers, physicians, and social workers—including the newly emergent psychiatric social workers—led the effort to institute the "advanced" method of caring for the mentally ill. A critical component of their publicity campaign was to identify their cause as "progressive" and enlightened, to urge San Franciscans to "go up" to the level of practice of cities like Boston and nations like Germany. By 1917, with the formation of the California Society for Mental Hygiene

35. Dr. Elmer E. Stone, "Report of the Medical Superintendent," 7 *St. Comm. Lun.* 1910, p. 60.
36. Dr. Robert L. Richards, "Report of the Medical Superintendent," 10 *St. Comm. Lun.* 1916, p. 86; F. W. Hatch, "The Need and Purposes of a Psychopathic Hospital," 9 *St. Comm. Lun.* 1914, p. 13.

in the city, the alliance of reformers had become publicly visible. By the end of the war heightened public concern over protecting community mental health provided the momentum that finally overcame the financial objections of the Board of Supervisors.

The elite reformers of San Francisco's Commonwealth Club were the first important local group to support the notion of the psychopathic ward. In a 1905 study of state charities the Club noted that "this state has a larger insane population than it ought to have" and that state hospitals made inadequate provision for "recent and more hopeful cases," mixing them indiscriminately with chronic incurables "in the basement, in the attic, and in 'shake downs' on the floor." A psychopathic hospital could hold "all hopeful cases . . . while there was still hope." A decade later Dr. Ray Lyman Wilbur addressed the Club's special session on the County Hospital Problem. "The San Francisco Hospital should provide . . . a psychopathic ward," Wilbur stressed, because "when I look over the people, active men in the community, mothers with children and large families who have been definitely insane at one time but who, with kind and considerate care, have completely recovered, I realize that we fail much in our duty in the way in which this community handles the problem of the mentally sick."[37] Not only would such a ward constitute a medically progressive innovation; it would also protect the reputations of responsible members of the community who succumbed to temporary breakdowns.

At the same meeting Dr. George Somers, a wealthy member of the San Francisco Board of Health, noted that

---

37. "Our State Charities," *Transactions of the Commonwealth Club of California* 1 (June 1905), 2-3; Dr. Ray Lyman Wilbur, "The County Hospital Problem," *Transactions of the Commonwealth Club of California* 10 (July 1915), 332-333. Dr. Wilbur's comments are especially interesting in revealing that a certain number of unnamed "active men in the community" had, in his opinion, "been definitely insane at one time."

"at present the insane [he was referring to persons charged with insanity] are confined in cells. . . . Shall the present system be perpetuated? It depends upon one's attitudes toward the insane. Are they mentally sick and in need of hospital treatment or are they possessed of a devil which needs only to be restrained? . . . Personally I believe they should be given hospital accommodations . . . either in a separate building on the San Francisco Hospital grounds or at least in a special ward." Unfortunately, he added, the city's Board of Health had not yet come to adopt his position.[38]

Elite reform bodies and certain leading physicians like Somers were actively behind the idea of a psychopathic ward by the middle of the second decade of the century. "Time and time again," complained a special report of the San Francisco Real Estate Board in 1916, "the need for better provision for the care of the insane has been pointed out by the superintendent of [San Francisco County] Hospital and representative physicians of the community. . . . Many persons now declared insane and sent to institutions would undoubtedly recover health and happiness if properly cared for . . . [in a] psychopathic ward." But the members of the Board of Health, who had succeeded only in 1912—after more than a decade of active pleading—in obtaining the Supervisors' approval for the three and a half million dollar hospital, were preoccupied with obtaining funding for the still-unconstructed tuberculosis and isolation wards. A psychopathic ward apparently did not appear to be a matter of equal urgency, probably because until 1919 there was a chance that the state legislature would establish (and finance) a psychopathic hospital in the city.[39]

38. Dr. George B. Somers, "The County Hospital Problem," pp. 319-320. Dr. Somers, who was now in 1915 urging the construction of a psychopathic ward, had been chairman of the Building Committee of the Board of Health in 1912—when it proposed a hospital complex lacking such a ward.
39. Bureau of Municipal Research (New York), *Report on a Survey of the*

In addition to the physicians and elite reformers, another smaller group of professionals—the psychiatric
social workers, who emerged in San Francisco just before
World War I—gave voice to the need for a psychopathic
ward. Psychiatric social work had begun in the city in
response to the growing desire of state hospital superintendents to "parole" those few patients for whom
family accommodations could be obtained. Dr. Eva Reid
headed the Bay Area "after-care department"—the first
in the state—which began its work in 1914 with a caseload of 117 parolees. In 1922 she had responsibility for
several psychiatric social workers and 202 parolees—out
of the state total of 792 parolees, which was 6 percent of
the total insane population of California's hospitals.

Yet as early as 1919, after only half a decade in aftercare, Dr. Reid came to the conclusion that her task was
bearing little fruit, since "many patients resent any sort
of follow-up work." Increasingly she turned to "preventative work," establishing in 1920 a psychiatric clinic—
one of four which emerged in the city during and after
the war. Approximately one-third of the 400 patients
she saw annually in the clinic were, she claimed, early
cases of "definite mental disease." Yet for those individuals "there is no treatment available in San Francisco," and since they were "in the early stages of the
disease," they were not, under the present law, "eligible

_____

Government of the City and County of San Francisco (San Francisco, 1916),
p. 471; Board of Supervisors, "Report of the Board of Health," San Francisco Municipal Reports (San Francisco, 1913), pp. 625-626. In April 1919
the state legislature passed a bill providing for a San Francisco Psychopathic
Hospital, but Governor Stevens, elected on an austerity platform, vetoed it
along with more than 200 other bills on May 27. Journal of the Assembly
During the 43rd Session of the Legislature of the State of California
(Sacramento, 1919), pp. 1189, 1584, 2128; Journal of the Senate During the
43rd Session of the Legislature of the State of California (Sacramento,
1919), p. 1961; "205 Bills Die by Governor's 'Pocket Veto,'" San Francisco
Examiner, May 28, 1919, p. 1.

for treatment in a state hospital." The only solution was a psychopathic ward in the city.[40]

The establishment in San Francisco, during and after the war, of four psychiatric clinics—not to mention four "psychological" clinics, two for children and two for adults—reveals not only the emergence of a new group of professionals, but also a growth of public support for "positive" or preventive mental hygiene. The active cultivation of mental hygiene had been urged by the National Committee for Mental Hygiene since its founding in 1908; in 1917 its affiliate, the California Society for Mental Hygiene, opened a clinic in San Francisco— the first on the West Coast. In its first ten months of operation, 445 patients applied for treatment.[41]

Social workers from the clinic devoted themselves to the treatment not only of disturbed individuals but of whole families, since they assumed that mental disorder stemmed in most cases from unhygienic conditions at home. This drive to cleanse the environment—common to other progressive campaigns—lent added weight to the argument in favor of a psychopathic ward. Social workers attached to the ward, it was argued, could strive to "re-educate the family" while doctors gave temporary restorative treatment to the disturbed individual; the

40. Dr. Eva C. Reid, "Report of the After-Care Physician," 1 *Cal. Dept. Instits.* 1923, p. 31; 7 *St. Bd. Char. and Corr.* 1916, p. 39; 10 *St. Bd. Char. and Corr.* 1923, pp. 44-45; "Report of the After-Care Physician," 12 *St. Comm. Lun.* 1920, pp. 25-27. The emergence of psychiatric social work in eastern cities can be followed in the following articles: Garnet Pelton, "The History and Status of Hospital Social Work," *Proceedings*, National Conference of Charities and Corrections, 1910, pp. 332-341, and Margherita Ryther, "Place and Scope of Psychiatric Social Work in Mental Hygiene," *Proceedings*, National Conference of Social Work, 1919 (Chicago, 1919), pp. 575-581.

41. Elsie Krafft, *The Mental Hygiene Clinic (from the standpoint of a social worker)* (San Francisco, 1918), p. 3. On the founding of the California Society for Mental Hygiene, see "Alienists Unite to Fight Lunacy," *San Francisco Examiner*, February 21, 1914, p. 3. For a list of members, see "Mental Hygiene Society," *Examiner*, June 6, 1915, p. 43.

afflicted person could then return to a healthier environment.[42]

The director of the California Society's mental hygiene clinic was Dr. Lillien Martin, professor emeritus of psychology at Stanford, who explained to an *Examiner* interviewer in 1917 that her "mission is to normalize the neurotic." Prominently displayed on the editorial page, the article surveyed what it described as a wave of psychotherapy in the city, and declared the phenomenon to be a predictable and salutary response to the malignant spread of neurosis among "citified" westerners. The writers praised Dr. Martin's struggle for mental hygiene, concluding that such work "makes a brighter promise to humanity than any other now engaging scientific thought."[43]

The *Examiner*, unlike the *Chronicle* or the *Call*, zealously pushed the psychopathic unit on its editorial page. A psychopathic facility, the paper urged in 1920, "will keep out of insane asylums folks who are not hopelessly unbalanced, but can be scientifically treated so as to make them again normal human beings capable of taking their place in society." It will "'make over' men and women who, left to themselves, become either charges upon

42. Krafft, *Mental Hygiene Clinic*, pp. 3-7. On the theory and practice of community mental hygiene at the national level, see especially C. Macfie Campbell, "The Mental Health of the Community and the Work of the Psychiatric Dispensary," and E. E. Southard, "Zones of Community Effort in Mental Hygiene," *Proceedings*, National Conference of Social Work, 1917 (Chicago, n.d.), pp. 429-438, 405-413. Both articles stress the role of the psychopathic hospital in the broad preventive effort. For a provocative critique of the drive by the "helping professions" to supervise and control internal family relationships since the early twentieth century, see Christopher Lasch, *Haven in a Heartless World: The Family Besieged* (New York, 1977). The social history of psychiatric social work remains to be written.

43. Bailey Miller, "How Psychology Will Normalize the Race," *San Francisco Examiner*, February 9, 1917, p. 16. See also the prior opinion piece submitted by one of the San Francisco Superior Court's medical examiners: Charles D. McGettigan, "Westerners Live Too Fast," *Examiner*, February 2, 1917, p. 11.

communities or inmates of penal and insanity institutions."[44]

After 1920 the appeals of medical professionals, lay reformers, psychiatric social workers, and the daily press combined into a steady, and frequently shrill, chorus; their tone became more urgent and uncompromising. An article by Mendocino Superintendent Richards in the *San Francisco Chronicle* was typical of the rhetoric of impending crisis. "Psychopathic hospitals are a vital necessity in California," he declared. "Most of the murders committed by the insane, the horrible crimes against children—to say nothing of the countless minor offenses—are manifestly not committed by the insane in mental hospitals." After catching the reader's attention with that hyperbole, he proceeded to point out that financial considerations alone were enough to prove the need. State costs for insane hospitals had topped three million dollars in 1920; the only way to avoid still higher costs was to treat persons with "abnormal mental personalities . . . earlier, when, in many notable instances, they could [be] cured and become valuable members of the community." The State Board of Health, which reprinted Richards' article in its weekly bulletin, agreed in urging that "as a matter of economy only, to say nothing of the humanitarian side of the case, psychopathic hospitals should be established in the large centers of population."[45]

The faculty of the School of Jurisprudence at the Uni-

44. "First Steps Taken in New Movement to Establish Psychopathic Hospital," Editorial, *San Francisco Examiner*, April 22, 1920, p. 22; "What is Expected of the Work of a State Psychopathic Hospital?," Editorial, *Examiner*, July 9, 1920, p. 20.

45. "Psychopathic Hospitals Would Save State Money," *California State Board of Health Weekly Bulletin* 1 (September 16, 1922), 2-3. The urgency expressed by medical superintendents after 1920 is no doubt partly the result of the difficulties they encountered between 1918 and 1920 in finding sufficient attendants, nurses, and doctors for their institutions; many of their employees entered military service or took higher-paying jobs elsewhere.

versity of California—not customarily a voice of reform
—likewise joined the chorus. In San Francisco "the handling of cases of persons mentally diseased is a disgrace to
our present-day civilization. . . . The detention home is a
jail, not a hospital. . . . The cost of maintenance is about
twelve thousand dollars a year, and the fees of the medical examiners are twelve thousand dollars more. With
this twenty-four thousand dollars the entire work could
be done reasonably well at the City and County Hospital.
. . . The worst evils can be corrected if the supervisors
will only appropriate the money." Moreover, as doctors
had been arguing for almost two decades, "preventive
treatment in the earlier stages in the majority of cases
saves the expense of commitment to the state hospital."[46]

The traditional psychiatric tenet that mental disease, if
treated in its early stages, would respond more success-
fully to medical treatment provided the theoretical under-
pinning for the establishment of psychopathic institutions. As a physician at Agnews State Hospital explained
in an article for a national journal, "the disorders of the
mind that ultimately culminate in what may be called
legal insanity—a condition in which the patient is dangerous to life and property—are frequently of slow and
insidious growth, so that often it is impossible to determine at just what point a peculiar personality ends and
disease begins. . . . It seems highly probable that we could
help such early cases if we could bring our assistance to
bear when their difficulties first arise." "Peculiar" behavior could be observed and treated in the psychopathic
ward before it had a chance to transform itself into
"disease."[47]

46. "Conduct of Insanity Proceedings," Editorial, 10 *California Law Review*, 226-228 (1922).

47. Dr. Henry S. Whisman, "Commitment Procedure and the State
Hospital," *Mental Hygiene* 7 (April 1923), 362. The national drive for the
psychopathic ward may be followed in these important articles: Dr. Adolf
Meyer, "Reception Hospitals, Psychopathic Wards, and Psychopathic Hospitals," *American Journal of Insanity* 64 (October 1907), 221-230; Dr.

In December 1923, the Board of Supervisors unanimously approved the establishment of a psychopathic ward at the San Francisco Hospital. Treatment would be limited to 15 days, a period which the supervisors considered adequate for "a complete diagnosis of mental condition." Physicians would have no trouble extending the two-week limit, however, since they could readmit any patient as many times as necessary. Treatment would, furthermore, be voluntary where possible, but involuntary where necessary, although in public the city authorities did not underscore the latter contingency. But as Dr. Harold Wright, President of the California Society for Mental Hygiene, put it in a closed meeting of the San Francisco Board of Health in 1921, "patients could be kept under observation even against their own consent by a simple matter of getting a warrant for them when the time had elapsed during which they were willing to stay."[48]

VI

The San Francisco Psychopathic Ward, as it emerged in the first quarter of the twentieth century, was a hybrid institution: in its primary function it was still a detention hospital, harboring those persons who, failing to respond to treatment, would be committed to a state hospital; in its secondary function it was a voluntary treatment facility for persons seeking medical help for

---

Albert M. Barrett, "Hospitals for the Acute and Recoverable Insane," *Proceedings*, National Conference of Charities and Corrections, 1907, pp. 397-411; Dr. Albert W. Ferris, "Psychopathic Wards in General Hospitals," *Proceedings*, National Conference of Charities and Corrections, 1910 (Ft. Wayne, Ind., 1910), pp. 264-275; Dr. James V. May, "The Functions of the Psychopathic Hospital," *American Journal of Insanity* 76 (July 1919), 21-34.

48. San Francisco Board of Supervisors, *Journal of Proceedings* 18 (December 10, 1923), 1271-1272; *State Board of Health Weekly Bulletin* 2 (December 29, 1923), 4-5; San Francisco Board of Health, *Minute Books*, October 20, 1921, p. 3124.

nervous or mental problems. In addition, it provided a laboratory for the study of mental disorders, to which classes from urban medical schools had easy access.

Since the Psychopathic Ward remained essentially a detention facility for persons awaiting commitment, the promised reduction in state expenditures for the insane —a prediction that medical professionals probably made in good faith—failed to take place, although the ward may conceivably have played a role in reducing the rate of increase in San Francisco commitments in the 1920s. The primary result of the emergence of the Psychopathic Ward, rather, was the extension of medical control over the commitment process. Doctors could now legally detain and treat "peculiar individuals"—who might in the absence of such treatment, they felt, become chronically "ill"—without needing to obtain court approval for the detention. If at the end of the two-week diagnostic period the patient was still irrational, he would be sent to the state hospital. No hearing would be necessary to inquire into his need for confinement; that need would already have been demonstrated by his failure to respond to two weeks of advanced treatment.

Doubtless some disturbed individuals benefited from this easier access to professional treatment. But others, subjected to treatment and in many cases commitment without either their consent or a true court hearing, may not have shared the doctors' assumption that "there is no longer so much danger that sane people will be deprived of their freedom as that insane people will not get the care they need in time for a fair chance of recovery."[49]

This basic assumption about the pathogenesis and ideal treatment of mental disorder—the conviction that early diagnosis would nip "acute" disturbances in the bud—was not based upon empirical investigation; no one sought to estimate how many untreated "acute" disorders were cured even without medical intervention.

49. 10 *St. Bd. Char. and Corr.* 1923, p. 23.

Recent studies have in fact suggested that early treatment sometimes makes a disorder worse. "Since many neurotic symptoms and fears are widely distributed and are transitory in nature," writes David Mechanic, "treating them as though they were aspects of emotional illness may . . . structure the symptom and the condition as part of [the patient's] self-identity and discourage him from attempting to cope with and overcome the problem."[50]

Medical professionals were no doubt sincere in their belief that such treatment would be beneficial. Their campaign to control the commitment process certainly did not originate in a self-conscious desire to deprive deviants of their liberty. Yet it is undeniable that the physicians' organized crusade for mental health tended to overlook the fact that commitment was indeed a deprivation of liberty. The caution expressed in the late nineteenth century by men like Dr. Stout and even by state hospital officials—who acknowledged that "railroading" was an ever-present danger—was no longer to be found in the medical literature and hospital reports of the early twentieth century. The suppression of this awareness within the medical profession after 1900 may have been a precondition for the aggressive, successful campaign to take control of the commitment process. Medical ideology—particularly the insistence on the necessity of medical intervention in acute cases—was determined to a large degree by the self-interest of doctors as a professional group. That ideology was admirably suited to building support for a major institutional innovation and for the expansion of their profession, both in power and in numbers.

Having succeeded in gaining control of the commitment process, physicians were no longer faced with the potential frustration of a court hearing, in which they

50. David Mechanic, *Mental Health and Social Policy* (Englewood Cliffs, N.J., 1969), pp. 27-28.

might have to demonstrate that the afflicted individual required forced "treatment." Such proof would indeed have been difficult to produce. For as the San Francisco case records suggest, a majority of those committed between 1906 and 1929—perhaps as many as two-thirds—exhibited no symptoms of severe disability or violent tendencies, which were the minimum legal requirements for commitment.

4

Routes to the Asylum: Commitments in San Francisco, 1900-1930

The two previous chapters examined the institutional and ideological developments that underlay the commitment process in California in the late nineteenth and early twentieth centuries. The "liberal" commitment policy followed by state officials beginning in the 1850s— the policy of incarcerating as "insane" thousands of burdensome deviants—had led by the early years of the twentieth century to a major crisis. State hospitals were bursting with patients, yet the legislature would no longer willingly finance more asylums. In response, state authorities simultaneously adopted two main lines of attack.

First, they launched a sterilization crusade—a decision that may only have compounded their difficulties, since to justify the campaign they had to publicize the threat seemingly posed by the mentally defective to the purity of the race. Such publicity, in turn, may have caused county judges and medical examiners to commit ever larger numbers of supposed defectives to asylums in order that they too might be rendered harmless.

Second, medical professionals led by state hospital officials agitated for the establishment of urban psychopathic wards—facilities that would provide doctors with the control they had long sought over the commitment process and thereby, it was argued, cause a reduction in the state hospital population. Proponents claimed that once doctors could handle incipient cases of mental disorder immediately and without interference by non-professionals, cures would multiply: the moderately sick would be restored to health and returned directly to the community without the stigma (and expense to the state) of lengthy asylum care.

Yet the campaign for the psychopathic ward, like the sterilization crusade, failed to fulfill its perceived promise. Of the five urban counties that had provided such wards by 1930—Alameda (Oakland), Fresno, Los Angeles, San Diego, and San Francisco—only the San Diego and San Francisco wards, according to an investigator from the State Department of Social Welfare, were "doing something more than merely keeping patients pending commitment." Only San Diego, moreover, was actively engaged in "treatment work." The San Francisco ward restricted its effort to "diagnosis rather than treatment."[1]

Meanwhile, the state hospital population, while not mounting as rapidly as the general population, continued to rise, contrary to the predictions of the medical professionals. Having reached 7,000 in 1910, 8,600 in 1912, and 9,300 in 1913, it leveled off at 10,000 through the war years and then climbed to 12,000 in 1922, 13,500 in 1926, and 15,000 by the end of the decade. Although San Francisco commitments did not keep pace with the increase in the adult population in the 1920s, a fact that may conceivably be related to the creation of the Psychopathic Ward, the city still provided an average of 570 per year, only slightly lower than the peak years between 1912 and 1920. San Francisco continued to supply about 30 percent of the total number of insane committed in California each year.

It was not only that the advocates of psychopathic

1. Frederick H. Allen, *Mental Hygiene Survey of the State of California* (Sacramento, 1932), pp. 142-143.

wards had exaggerated the ease of curing in short order those persons admitted with disturbances that may in principle have been treatable. More importantly, they had failed to understand—or if they understood, to acknowledge—the actual role that local authorities, with the acquiescence of the state legislature, implicitly commanded the new wards, like the old state hospitals, to play. For decades the California state government had made it easy for local communities to dump a wide variety of burdensome deviants on state institutions. What doctors and other reformers in their zealous campaigning for the psychopathic ward had either failed to note or chosen to overlook was that this traditional statewide method of dealing with troublesome individuals was still intact. Although medical professionals had won the authority to decide for or against long-term commitment without overt lay interference, they did not have the power, sought by specialists in diseases of the mind, to strictly limit admissions to persons with "well-defined" mental disorders. Local community authorities could still see to it that the psychopathic ward, the state hospitals, and the physicians that manned them, remained dedicated to the broader, traditional goal: the confinement of individuals who, whether mentally ill or not, seemed to threaten family stability or public tranquility.

Medical men, though united in their drive to eliminate lay interference in the commitment process, were therefore seriously divided on the issue of where in practice to draw the line between the sane and the insane. The general practitioners appointed by the county courts to serve as medical examiners were content to follow traditional practices. Like the local community officials they served, they accepted the psychopathic ward, but on the condition that it not interfere with a broad commitment policy. Physicians working at the state level, as well as some local specialists in psychological medicine, tried

unsuccessfully to limit admissions to clear-cut mental
cases. Of course they did not believe that sane deviants
ought to roam uncontrolled; they simply wished that the
counties, in the absence of a state almshouse, would
confine them in local institutions. But the combined
political weight of the counties—each of which had a
common interest in dumping local undesirables on the
state—continued to dwarf the power of the state-level
physicians. The state legislature showed no interest in
forcing the counties to detain non-mental cases locally.

The San Francisco commitment records reveal that for
that metropolis at any rate, the liberal policy went un-
challenged at least up to 1929, the last year for which
court records were available. Although the *numbers* of
deviants committed through the San Francisco Superior
Court did not keep pace with population in the 1920s—
partly in response, it seems, to the availability of outpatient treatment at several urban clinics—the *types*
committed remained unchanged. The "insane" continued
to comprise not just those with well-defined mental
diseases, but the traditionally wide array of deviants as
well.

The creation of the San Francisco Psychopathic Ward
in 1923 did not directly affect most persons charged with
insanity. Only a small proportion of those committed—
less than 20 percent in any year up to 1930—passed
through the Psychopathic Ward at all. But the observation of some detainees at the Psychopathic Ward served
the vital function of helping to legitimize the entire
commitment system. For with the establishment of the
ward, it could be argued that a decisive safeguard had
been built into the system. Any allegedly insane person
about whose illness there was the slightest doubt could
be treated for up to two weeks—allegedly without any
stigma—in a local facility, where he would benefit from
the latest advances in diagnosis and therapy. If at the end
of that time he showed no improvement, there would be

no doubt about the advisability of committing him for an indefinite period to a state hospital. Failure to respond to the sophisticated treatment ordered by the Psychopathic Ward would amount to ipso facto proof of the need for confinement.

This chapter and the two following chapters will examine in detail the commitment system in San Francisco in the first three decades of the twentieth century. Focusing on one city—a metropolis that supplied the state with almost one-third of its insane population—allows us to view institutional, ideological, and professional developments from the standpoint of concrete commitment decisions. In addition, studying a large group of the insane through individual court records permits us to grasp how strikingly heterogeneous a group they were. Individuals committed for insanity shared neither a common social background, a similar mental condition, nor even a customary "route" to the asylum. What united them, instead, was a type of relationship to other people. The insane were disturbing, peculiar, or incomprehensible. They were in many cases out of touch with reality and in a small number of cases violent or destructive. But they became insane not when they crossed some well-defined boundary between health and sickness, between normality and abnormality. They became insane when other individuals decided they could no longer be tolerated.

I will look first, in the remainder of this chapter, at the routes the insane took to the asylum, the various paths along which more than 12,000 San Franciscans were carried to one of four state hospitals in northern California between 1906 and 1929—the years for which I was able to obtain San Francisco Superior Court records. Chapters Five and Six will focus respectively on the social backgrounds of the insane and on their allegedly insane behavior.

II

The route to the asylum began with the petition of any person in the community willing to swear that the allegedly insane individual was "so far disordered in mind" that he was "dangerous to be at large." Once an official affidavit was filed in court, the person so accused would be conducted, usually by a sheriff's deputy, to the thirteen-cell Detention Hospital for the Insane. Adjoining Jefferson Square at the corner of Gough Street and Golden Gate Avenue, the Detention Hospital was a small wooden structure erected in 1895 and rebuilt after the 1906 earthquake. At its unveiling it was hailed as a progressive step in the humanitarian care of the insane, who previously had often been detained at the county jail pending a decision on their sanity. Yet the Detention Hospital itself, as numerous observers pointed out in the early twentieth century, so completely "reproduced the jail atmosphere both in appearance of the wards and in the care provided" that it was "a jail in all but name."[2]

Until 1923, when the San Francisco Hospital's thirty-bed Psychopathic Ward opened, the alleged insane spent between one and seven days—the legal limit was five—at the Detention Hospital. After one or two days of confinement, two court-appointed medical examiners would spend a few minutes with the accused, listen to the accounts of "witnesses," and then make their recommendation to the Superior Court judge—a recommendation that in the 23 years covered by available records the presiding judge chose to reject in only four cases.

After 1923, a small proportion of detainees spent an additional 12 to 14 days at the Psychopathic Ward, located a few miles away in the Potrero District. An exami-

2. Bureau of Municipal Research (New York), *Report on a Survey of the Government of the City and County of San Francisco* (San Francisco, 1916), p. 471; "Municipal Research Bureau Scores S.F. Methods," *San Francisco Call*, October 29, 1916, p. 23; Allen, *Mental Hygiene Survey of the State of California*, p. 138.

nation of all case records for 1925, 1927, and 1929 reveals that only 12 percent, 11 percent, and 17 percent, respectively, of those brought to the Detention Hospital and subsequently committed passed any time at the Psychopathic Ward. Even those who did still returned to the Detention Hospital before leaving for the state hospital. Hence, all of those committed prior to 1923 and the vast majority committed after that date spent only a few days in custody—in the locked cells of the Detention Hospital —before being conducted by sheriff's deputy to a state hospital at Agnews (San Jose), Napa, Mendocino, or Stockton.

While all of those committed passed through the city's Detention Hospital, the paths they took to get there varied enormously. A few examples will illustrate how diverse those routes were. In the summer of 1906 the San Francisco police arrested a 52-year-old Canadian-born vagrant for "wandering about the streets." Judging the man's behavior "irrational," they took him to the Detention Hospital. After one night in his cell the medical examiner checked him, noting only that he was "quiet, refuses to answer questions." Despite his silence, however, he was clearly, in the examiner's opinion, "unable to care for himself." The doctor recommended commitment and the following day—48 hours after the police picked him up—a sheriff's deputy escorted him to the Napa State Hospital, where he would remain confined at least three months, and perhaps a good deal longer.[3]

In 1909 a 35-year-old native-born Californian, a woman with no occupation, was charged with insanity on

3. It was not possible to determine exactly how long sample members remained in state hospitals after commitment. In 1925, however, the Director of the Psychopathic Ward at San Francisco General Hospital stated that "a case is always kept in those asylums at least three months." In earlier years the minimum period of stay would probably have been at least that long, if not longer. San Francisco Department of Public Health, *Minute Books*, February 19, 1925, p. 3677.

an affidavit signed by a welfare official of the Associated Charities. The examiners reported that she had been to the Detention Hospital "repeatedly" in the past, the last time "wearing a sailor's uniform," and that she "is a public nuisance" on account of her "foul language." While in detention, they noted, she even "calls the attendants names." She had been "acting strangely since the earthquake" three years before, and this time the examiners decided her behavior could no longer be tolerated. She was sent the following day to Agnews State Hospital.

The same year a mother swore that her 18-year-old son, a high-school graduate with no occupation, was insane. The medical examiners wrote that he "lacks interest in affairs, lacks affection for mother and relatives, lacks initiative, is not interested in his personal appearance or his future." His mother also claimed that he once "took his uncle's pistol and fired five shots in the house," and that his insanity had begun "in childhood." The examiners gave him a diagnosis of dementia praecox (schizophrenia) and the judge committed him two days later to the Stockton State Hospital.

In 1910 a 35-year-old Englishman, who had been in California since 1893, walked into the Detention Hospital of his own accord. The examiners noted that he "talks rationally, seeks treatment for opium habit"— which he had had for three years. They recommended commitment and he was sent to the Mendocino State Hospital.

In 1920 a 25-year-old prostitute was examined at the Detention Hospital after a County Hospital doctor testified by affidavit that she had "persistently refused" treatment for "lues" (syphilis). The examiner added that she "is a high-class moron, has been in trouble ever since the age of 14, is a prostitute and a menace to society." Those facts persuaded the judge to commit her to Napa State Hospital.

In 1924 a 53-year-old Irish-born domestic was brought

to the Detention Hospital on a petition signed by a cousin. She had been committed to state hospitals twice before, in 1910 and 1914, after having threatened to kill herself and having suffered from "delusions of persecution." The examiners noted that "she has never been well since first commitment," that she had insane relatives, and that she was "morose, sulky, and jealous." The following day she was sent back to Stockton for the third time.

In 1927 a 47-year-old Russian-born lumberman, married and a resident of San Francisco for 17 years, was detained after his wife charged that he "became very religious, would stay on knees constantly." Sent for observation to the Psychopathic Ward, he was "noisy and combative," whereupon he was returned to the Detention Hospital and commited to Napa.

The same year a 40-year-old Russian-born housewife was detained after her husband claimed that "she makes foolish purchases." The examiners noted that "patient and friends deny all accusations made by husband," and that "marital difficulties seem to figure in the case," so they decided to "parole" her to a private hospital for treatment. But three days later she was back at the Detention Hospital, apparently having become worse while at the private hospital. After one additional day in detention, the judge committed her to Napa State Hospital.

III

The routes to the asylum, as these illustrations indicate, varied to some extent in the length of detention prior to commitment and in the number of hospitals or agencies the individual passed through during that period. But they varied most significantly in terms of the identity of the initial petitioner. Some of the insane came to the court because family members, friends, neighbors, or employers with whom they had daily contact considered them no longer tolerable; others were detained because doctors, police, or charity personnel—with whom they may have had little or no prior contact—judged them irrational. A statistical analysis of the San Francisco records allows us to focus in detail upon the initial accusation of insanity. We can determine which groups—relatives, doctors, police, and others—petitioned the courts with the greatest frequency and whether the type of accuser varied according to the social characteristics of the accused.[4]

The most common petitioners, in order of frequency, were relatives, doctors, police, friends, neighbors, relief home administrators, charity workers, and employers. The relatives comprised 57 percent, doctors 21 percent, and police 8 percent; these three groups made up more than four-fifths of the total. In all, one-third of the insane were accused initially by persons acting in an official or professional capacity—doctors, police, charity workers and administrators, or court personnel.

Yet each category of petitioners did not contribute a constant share over the entire period covered by the San Francisco records (Table 3). While relatives accused a

4. Superior Court of the City and County of San Francisco, *Records of Commitments for Insanity*, May 1906 to May 1929, 63 volumes, San Francisco City and County Records Center. From the original records covering 12,150 consecutive commitments between May 1906 and May 1929, I drew a systematic sample of 1,229 cases, comprising every fifth "patient" in each of the twelve even-numbered years between 1906 and 1928 (the "1906" cases included all those admitted between May 19, 1906, and May 18, 1907). A sample of 1,229 cases yields highly reliable conclusions: 99 out of 100 random samples of that size will have an error range of less than 4 percent, and 95 out of 100 will err by less than 3 percentage points. As a test of the reliability of the sample, I recorded the nativity of each member of the entire insane population from 1906 to 1928: 25.5 percent were born in California (vs. 25.3 percent of the sample), 26.3 percent were born in other parts of the United States (vs. 27.2 percent of the sample), 7.7 percent were born in Ireland (vs. 7.7 percent), 6.9 percent in Germany (vs. 6.9 percent), and 5.7 percent in Italy (vs. 5.1 percent). The sample percentages of these and every other nativity group err by less than 1 percent.

Table 3

DISTRIBUTION OF COMMITTED PERSONS, BY IDENTITY OF PETITIONER
CHARGING THEM WITH INSANITY, 1906-1916, 1918-1928, AND 1906-1928

Petitioners by category	Percent charged 1906-1916		Percent charged 1918-1928		Percent charged 1906-1928	
Relatives	(n=252)	53.5	(n=385)	59.3	(n=637)	56.9
Doctors	(n=88)	18.7	(n=149)	23.0	(n=237)	21.2
Police	(n=63)	13.4	(n=24)	3.7	(n=87)	7.8
Other official personnel*	(n=14)	3.0	(n=32)	4.9	(n=46)	4.1
Other personal relations†	(n=54)	11.5	(n=59)	9.1	(n=113)	10.1
	(n=471)	100.1	(n=649)	100.0	(n=1120)	100.1
Unidentifiable petitioners	81		28		109	
Total number of petitions	552 (44.9%)		677 (55.1%)		1229 (100%)	

*Charity workers, relief home or hospital employees, court personnel.
† Friends, neighbors, employers, landlords.

growing proportion between 1906 and 1928 and doctor
and "other official" affidavits also increased somewhat,
the proportion of police accusations fell markedly.
Whereas in the decade from 1906 to 1916 45 percent of
the total number of commitments took place, almost
three-fourths of all police accusations—compared to less
than 40 percent of the doctor and other official affidavits—were issued in the same period. The drop in
police affidavits was probably even greater, since many
of the unidentifiable petitioners—who were almost three
times as frequent in the first decade—could well have
been policemen (doctors' names were prefaced with
"Dr." and relatives frequently had the same surname as
the accused).

Clearly, by the 1920s the police were less likely to
perform the official act of being the first to charge an
individual with insanity. The police still continued, as
they do today, to apprehend deviants—including many
of the alleged insane—and take them to an emergency
hospital, thus initiating the commitment process.[5] But
the specific task of attesting to insane behavior was
passing increasingly into the hands of medical and social
work professionals with special training in the diagnosis
of "mental illness."

It is nevertheless revealing to examine more closely
those individuals officially charged by the police—a
group committed largely before the First World War.
For these insane persons were in all likelihood representative of the much larger group of cases "initiated" by
the police both before and after the war.

Whom did the police accuse, and by extension, whom
did they apprehend and conduct to the emergency hospital? In the first place, they petitioned for the commit-

5. See Egon Bittner, "Police Discretion in Emergency Apprehension of
Mentally Ill Persons," *Social Problems* 14 (Winter 1967), 278-292, a study
of the contemporary role of police in conducting those suspected of mental
illness to a detention hospital in a large northern California city.

ment of foreign-born individuals twice as often as for native-born persons. They signed the affidavits of 10 percent of all foreign-born insane, but of only 5 percent of the native-born. Put a different way, while just under half of the insane were foreign-born (48 percent), more than 60 percent of those accused by police were foreign-born. The police also accused men more often than women, and the young more frequently than the old. More than 80 percent of the police affidavits went to men, though males made up less than 60 percent of the insane. Of all sample members aged 20 to 29, one in ten was accused by the police, compared with one in twelve of those between 30 and 49 and one in twenty of those over 50. Police affidavits likewise stand out disproportionately among the unmarried, and among those who had resided in California for less than five years.

Of course, those persons who were least likely to have relatives in San Francisco (the foreign-born, the men, the unmarried, and the recent arrivals) were the most likely to be committed by non-relatives, including the police. More than 80 percent of those with police affidavits had no relatives in the city (no relatives, that is, that the Superior Court could locate), whereas less than 40 percent of the insane as a group lacked relatives in the city.

Yet the lack of relatives probably does not in the end explain why the foreign-born were so disproportionately accused by the police. For if we compare the foreign-born to those born in America but outside California, we find that while the foreign-born were considerably more likely to be charged by police, they were just as likely as the non-Californian natives to have relatives in San Francisco. In addition, the foreign-born were equally likely to be older, to be married, and to have resided for more than five years in California. The only exception to this pattern is sex: the foreign-born were slightly more likely than the non-Californians to be men. Although the number of cases is too small for a high degree of statistical significance, they still suggest the strong possibility that being foreign-born in itself increased one's chances of being accused of insanity by the police.

In the concrete, of course, nativity did not ordinarily operate as an independent social characteristic. It is especially difficult to distinguish the effects of nativity from those of occupation, since the foreign-born insane— like the rest of the foreign-born—were more heavily concentrated in blue-collar positions than the native-born. Eighty-four percent of the foreign-born insane were blue-collar, compared to 68 percent of the native-born. More than 30 percent of the foreign-born insane were unskilled, against less than 20 percent of the natives.[6]

Was it in fact their occupational level that led the foreign-born into more frequent contact with, and accusations by, the police? If so, then we would expect native-born blue-collar workers to have an equal proportion of police affidavits. In fact, they have a much smaller proportion. Of the 242 foreign-born sample members with blue-collar occupations and identifiable petitioners, 15 percent were accused by the police; of the 239 native-born sample members in those categories, 9 percent were committed on police affidavits. In the semi-skilled and unskilled ranks, which included 188 foreign-born and 163 native-born sample members, 16 percent of the foreigners but only 7 percent of the natives were accused by police. It would of course be useful to be able to determine whether more foreign-born white-collar workers were accused by police than native-born, but so few foreign insane belonged to that occupational category that we cannot adequately hold nativity constant. It seems likely, nevertheless, that foreign birth was a more

6. Each sample member was assigned to the white-collar or blue-collar category in accordance with the detailed coding scheme developed by Stephan Thernstrom and discussed in detail in the next chapter.

significant determinant of a police accusation than occupational position.

A reading of the individual court cases suggests the explanation that the foreign-born were more liable to engage in public behavior that the police considered irrational—behavior which may or may not have been so clearly irrational from the standpoint of the person's own native culture. Often the court records reveal only that the individual was picked up for "wandering in the streets," or for "irrational behavior"—as in the case of a 41-year-old Japanese man who in 1908 was "acting irrationally in the street" and was brought to the Detention Hospital. While at the hospital he was quiet, yet he believed, in the medical examiner's words, that "someone [was] persecuting him." That "delusion" was cited as evidence of the man's insanity, despite the fact that his feeling of persecution may well have emerged from his treatment at the hands of the police or hospital personnel themselves.

So many foreigners were arrested for "irrational" wandering that one begins to suspect that the foreign-born may simply not have understood as well as natives did the propensity of the police to apprehend persons strolling without "business" in the streets—perhaps especially in fashionable neighborhoods. An Irish laborer, for example, "was brought to the Detention Hospital by a police officer who found him wandering about Ingleside Terrace"—a fashionable residential area near Twin Peaks. According to the police, he "kept on walking" and "would not answer questions." The medical examiner noted that the man was "nervous" while in detention, but cited no other behavior as evidence of insanity. The following day the judge committed him to Agnews State Hospital. In a similar case, an illiterate Greek laborer was "picked up by police wandering aimlessly around Golf Links"—another middle-class stronghold by the Presidio. He was "very filthy," "confused," and "talked irrationally." At the Detention Hospital the examiners noted they were "unable to get reliable answers." Two days later the judge sent him to Napa.[7]

Furthermore, once apprehended, the foreigner may have had more difficulty giving a satisfactory account of himself, if only for reasons of language. Typical of many others in the sample was a 49-year-old Italian laborer, "picked up by the police, acting very irrationally" in 1926, who was "unable to give a clear account of himself, doesn't seem to understand questions asked, nor does he give rational answers. He answers 'don't know' to all that is asked."

In other cases the police described the foreigner's behavior more specifically. In 1908, for example, a 34-year-old Peruvian "merchant" who had been in the United States only six weeks was "arrested on the street for acting strangely; he was on his knees praying, making gestures, etc." In Peru, one might suppose, such spontaneous public worship may not have signified an unbalanced mind. In 1910 a German-born laborer went to the police station itself "complaining of being ejected from society." The police reported to the medical examiner that the man lectured them on socialism, leading the physician to conclude that he was suffering from "delu-

7. Philippe Ariès has noted that in modern society the "middle class could no longer bear the pressure of the multitude or the contact of the lower class. It seceded . . . to organize itself separately . . . in new districts kept free from all lower-class contamination." Many of those foreigners arrested in San Francisco for "wandering in the streets" were products of more traditional cultures—in which, as Ariès observes of southern Italy, the daily intermingling of rich and poor persisted into the twentieth century. Ariès, *Centuries of Childhood: A Social History of Family Life*, trans. Robert Baldick (New York, 1965), pp. 414-415. In American cities in the early twentieth century—as Sam Bass Warner, Jr., has pointed out—neighborhoods were segregated not only by class but by ethnicity. Unskilled workers, who were disproportionately foreign-born, were particularly "ghettoized." Warner, *The Private City* (Philadelphia, 1968), p. 169. One wonders how many of the foreigners picked up for "irrational wandering" were in fact picked up in neighborhoods where they clearly did not "belong."

sions of a socialistic nature." In 1925 another German, a 51-year-old baker, was arrested for vagrancy after losing his job. The examiners wrote that according to the police he "is a soap-box orator and is a Socialist." They added: "Wanders about streets and is noisy and disturbs peace and has unlimited nerve getting on without work." After one day in detention he was conducted to Mendocino. In Germany, a laborer zealously pleading the socialist cause, on a soap box or even in a police station, might have been considered rational, even if foolish or offensive. The cultural backgrounds of the foreign-born insane, in sum, appear to offer at least a partial explanation for their disproportionate representation among those accused by the San Francisco police. It is also conceivable, of course, that the police may in general have tended to consider foreigners—especially recent immigrants— more "bothersome" than natives regardless of their actual behavior.

Doctors—the primary group of "official" accusers— were, like the police, more likely to accuse men, the unmarried, the recent arrivals in the state, and those without relatives in the city. As in the case of police accusations, eight in ten of those accused by doctors lacked relatives in the city.

But although the police and doctors might appear at first glance to have been accusing an identical group of unattached male non-Californians, important differences emerge when we distinguish nativity, sex, and age. Whereas all foreign nativity groups appeared to be equally represented in the police accusations—though the number of cases was too small to be absolutely sure— the Irish, most numerous of the non-American-born, were curiously underrepresented in the doctor accusations and overrepresented among those committed by relatives (Table 4).

Less than 15 percent of the Irish insane were accused by doctors, compared to at least 23 percent of every other

Table 4

PERCENT OF COMMITTED PERSONS CHARGED WITH INSANITY BY
RELATIVES AND DOCTORS, BY NATIVITY GROUP, 1906-1929

Birthplace		Charged by Relatives	Charged by Doctors
Ireland	(n=82)	70.7	14.6
Germany	(n=74)	51.4	27.0
Italy	(n=56)	48.2	23.2
Scandinavia	(n=68)	26.8	29.4
Other Southern and Eastern Europe	(n=47)	44.6	27.7
Asia and Mexico	(n=44)	34.1	29.5
Other foreign	(n=143)	46.2	23.8
California	(n=281)	79.4	10.3
Other U.S.	(n=297)	52.5	24.9

foreign nativity group. The Irish were among the oldest immigrant groups to settle in California, to be sure, and were much more likely to have relatives—especially children—in the city than any other foreign-born group. On the other hand, the California-born received almost as many doctor affidavits as the Irish yet had a much higher proportion of relatives than the Irish: only 12 percent of the native Californians were reported to have no kin in the city, compared to 25 percent of the Irish. Clearly there was no simple correlation between the proportion of relatives in the city and the proportion of affidavits signed by relatives. Either the Irish were much more reluctant than other groups to appeal to the authority of medical personnel when a relative seemed disturbed, or other variables are intervening.

Two other characteristics—age and especially sex— appear to hold the key to an explanation. For what distinguishes the San Francisco Irish, sane or insane, from all other nationalities is their high proportion of women and old people. The 1930 federal census reveals that the Irish were the only major nationality group in San Francisco with more women than men. Of the 16,508 Irish-born residents of the city, 51 percent were female. Among the 18,360 Germans, 42 percent were women, and among the 26,898 Italians, only 38 percent were female. The Mexicans, Central Americans, and Australians were the other groups with a slight preponderance of women, but none contributed more than 1,600 residents to the population.

Furthermore, 17 percent of the Irish in San Francisco were over the age of 65, as were 21 percent of the Germans and 6 percent of the Italians; 11 percent of the city's population was over 65. If it were possible to determine the sex of the aged persons in each nationality group, we would in all likelihood find that the Irish supplied a very disproportionate share of the city's aged females.[8]

Table 5 shows that while 58 percent of all sample members were men, only 45 percent of the Irish were men. One-third of the Irish were over 60 years of age, and one-sixth over 70, compared to one-eighth and one-twentieth of the total sample. Among all those accused by doctors, moreover, only 20 percent were women. And among the aged, although the number of cases is small, doctor petitions appear to have been disproportionately few—especially among women, but also among men—regardless of nationality.

Why, then, should doctors have accused women, and possibly the aged, less frequently than men and the young? It seems unlikely, in the first place, that in the

8. Department of Commerce, Bureau of the Census, *Fifteenth Census of the United States, 1930, Population*, vol. 2 (Washington, D.C., 1933), pp. 833, 1088. Earlier census reports did not include a cross-tabulation of sex and age by nationality group.

Table 5

PERCENT OF COMMITTED PERSONS WHO WERE FEMALE,
AND OF COMMITTED PERSONS WHO WERE OVER AGE 60,
BY NATIVITY GROUP, 1906-1929

Birthplace		Female		Over 60
Ireland	(n=92)	55.4	(n=88)	33.0
Germany	(n=82)	41.5	(n=80)	21.3
Italy	(n=61)	37.7	(n=59)	8.5
Scandinavia	(n=75)	29.3	(n=72)	11.2
Other Southern and Eastern Europe	(n=57)	35.1	(n=52)	9.5
Asia and Mexico	(n=47)	19.1	(n=42)	7.2
Other foreign	(n=155)	38.1	(n=148)	13.6
California	(n=302)	47.7	(n=299)	1.6
Other U.S.	(n=325)	44.3	(n=316)	16.4

early twentieth century American women and old people exhibited any particular reluctance to consult physicians; nor does it seem likely that their relatives should have hesitated to appeal to doctors for advice when they manifested signs of mental disturbance. On the contrary, it seems plausible that relatives felt considerably freer, in the case of women and the aged, to step forward publicly themselves in accusation. Medical sanction for that momentous public act may not have seemed quite as necessary as it did in the case of a younger male. As we shall see in greater detail in the next chapter, Americans had apparently for decades commonly assumed that women possessed an innately nervous constitution and that old age naturally signified a diminished capacity to reason or perform a functional social role. Both women and the aged, many medical and lay observers held, were particularly prone to contract nervous or mental disorders.

Relatives may therefore have assumed more readily that the old or the female, when disturbed, required a period of confinement—and women and the aged may often have shared that assumption.

It is perhaps not being too cynical to suggest, furthermore, that children and others with a financial stake in family property may sometimes have had an interest in recommending confinement of an elder relative, who would at that point be subject to guardianship proceedings and loss of the right to hold property. At any rate, the proclivity of Irish relatives for the role of petitioner would seem to be determined not by aversion to professional medical consultation, but rather by which Irish were "ill." This is not to say that Irish women or Irish old people were either more disturbed or more disturbing to relatives than their counterparts in other nationality groups. It is only to say that the Irish insane—who, like the Irish in the general population, were disproportionately female and disproportionately aged—may for that reason have been confined more frequently on affidavits signed by relatives than by doctors.

In one other important respect, the pattern of petitioning—the first official step in the commitment process—displayed an important variation by nationality group. Once accused of insanity, individuals born in the United States were much more likely than foreigners to declare that they would go "voluntarily" to the state hospital. One out of every twenty persons charged with insanity expressed a willingness, according to the medical examiner, to go to the state hospital voluntarily.[9] But

9. These individuals must be distinguished from the entirely different group—an average of about 30 annually—who after 1911 circumvented the court procedure altogether by committing themselves to a state hospital under the "voluntary admission" program. Those in this latter group were still legally committed—they could in fact only leave the hospital when the medical superintendent decided to release them—but they did not go through the court and therefore are not included in the court commitment

of the approximately 25 individuals committed "voluntarily" through the San Francisco court each year, more than 80 percent were native-born. Not a single Italian, Eastern European, Asian, or Mexican—groups contributing more than 150 persons to the sample of 1,229 insane—availed himself of the opportunity. Moreover, 80 percent of the voluntary patients were men, and a somewhat disproportionate one-half were Protestant—a religious affiliation claimed by only 40 percent of the sample members. Even the unskilled among the native Protestants supplied their proportionate share, suggesting that occupational position has no effect. These facts do not prove that the native-born, the male, or the Protestant were more willing to accept the prospect of psychiatric treatment than the foreign-born, the female, or the Catholic. But they do suggest that the latter groups were less likely to express to the medical examiners a readiness to be confined indefinitely in a state hospital.[10]

A clear majority of all petitioners, as previously noted, were relatives of the individual committed—a fact that plainly reveals the centrality of family relationships in the insanity labeling process. Eighty percent of the native Californians received affidavits from relatives, as did 70 percent of the Irish and approximately one-half of the

---

records. The figure of 30 voluntary admissions each year is an estimate obtained by taking the total number of voluntary admissions in northern California, and multiplying it by the fraction of total admissions—voluntary and involuntary—supplied by San Francisco. This method assumes that each county provided an identical proportion of involuntary and voluntary patients.

10. Published state statistics of mental hospital admissions for the years 1911 to 1928 reveal that women were also underrepresented in the 3,500 "voluntary" admissions statewide that bypassed the court. Women comprised 44 percent of those admissions, but 47 percent of the state's population between 1910 and 1930. (Figures calculated from data in annual reports of the State Commission in Lunacy, State Department of Institutions, and Federal Census Bureau population reports.)

Germans, Italians, and native-born non-Californians. Most insane persons, therefore, were family members whose behavior was no longer tolerable to the rest of the family. Through the insane commitment procedure, the government in effect "socialized" such troubling behavior, relieving relatives of the real burden and in most cases of the cost of caring for a family member whom they considered disturbed. Some families, no doubt, would have been willing to tolerate deviant relatives were it not for the financial burden of caring for them. But by subsidizing only institutional, and not "outdoor," relief for disturbed individuals, the state forced those families to turn to commitment proceedings.

Table 6 reveals which relatives were the most common among the identifiable petitioners. For the most part, petitioning relatives were spouses and siblings.

Table 6

DISTRIBUTION OF RELATIVES WHO PETITIONED FOR
THE COMMITMENT OF A FAMILY MEMBER, 1906-1929

Relative		*As percent of all petitioners*	*As percent of petitioning relatives*
Husbands	(n=163)	14.6	25.7
Wives	(n=77)	6.9	12.1
Sisters	(n=87)	7.8	13.7
Brothers	(n=81)	7.2	12.7
Mothers	(n=54)	4.8	8.4
Fathers	(n=36)	3.2	5.6
Daughters	(n=33)	2.9	5.1
Sons	(n=27)	2.4	4.2
Others	(n=79)	7.1	12.5
		56.9	100.0

However, among those committed by spouses, the person charged was considerably more likely to be a wife than a husband. Although wives comprised a somewhat higher proportion of the insane population (20 percent) than husbands (15 percent), the disproportion is still striking: husbands accused wives more than twice as often as wives accused husbands. It would appear that the commitment of a married man was more likely to require the intervention of a male authority at the stage of initial accusation—a doctor, a brother, or a son.

IV

Between 70 and 85 percent of those individuals held during any given year at the Detention Hospital were in fact ultimately committed to a state hospital. As recent investigators have discovered in analyzing contemporary commitment proceedings, the initial charge of insanity is much more likely to be upheld by urban courts than it is to be dismissed. For example, Thomas Scheff's research on Wisconsin in the early 1960s showed that urban courts nearly always rubber-stamped the prior judgment of family members or other petitioners that the disturbed person required hospitalization. Urban courts, he concluded, conducted such a volume of business that there was no time to screen patients with care.[11]

In early twentieth-century San Francisco, as in many localities today, the standard practice of paying the examiner a flat fee for each examination likewise put a premium on the speed with which he could dispose of each case.[12] To conduct a thorough investigation of the

11. Thomas Scheff, "Social Conditions for Rationality: How Urban and Rural Courts Deal with the Mentally Ill," *American Behavioral Scientist* 7 (March 1964), 21-27.

12. San Francisco medical examiners received five dollars per examination, allowing them to earn a minimum of $150 a month for less than one hour of work per day in 1901, and a minimum of $250 for the same amount of work in 1923. It is hardly surprising that 40 or more local physicians applied to fill the vacancy that occurred in 1915. "Litigation May Follow

social or familial context of the individual's behavior—
which might have made apparently bizarre behavior
seem more reasonable—would have required quite a considerable expenditure of time.[13]

Medical assumptions about disease also tended to increase the likelihood that a disturbed individual already
in detention would be committed. Physicians were, and
are, clearly biased in favor of treating individuals who
exhibited symptoms, rather than not treating them. As
Scheff has expressed it, the medical profession has his-
torically committed itself to the view that "judging a sick
person well is more to be avoided than judging a well
person sick." By this reasoning, premature release would
constitute a graver risk than unnecessary confinement.[14]

It was therefore in keeping with the canons of professional medicine to recommend commitment at the slightest indication of disturbed behavior. A cursory examination could be easily justified, furthermore, by an appeal
to the then-current psychiatric assumption that while
the present condition of the accused might be ambigu-
ous, progressive deterioration was likely and immediate
treatment therefore indispensable; a clearer diagnosis
could be established after the patient had been in the
state hospital for a time. The assumption of a progressive, often quite gradual, deterioration thus permitted

Ruling," *San Francisco Call*, December 14, 1901, p. 8; "Dr. McElroy Named
on Lunacy Board, Choice Unanimous," *San Francisco Examiner*, September
5, 1923, p. 17; "Sturtevant Takes Rich Plum from Confreres," *San Francisco
Chronicle*, January 5, 1915, p. 4.

13. Two recent significant reports on the "non-clinical" determinants of
the courtroom decision for commitment are Dorothy Miller and Michael
Schwartz, "County Lunacy Commission Hearings: Some Observations of
Commitments to a State Mental Hospital," *Social Problems* 14 (Summer
1966), 26-35; and Werner M. Mendel and Samuel Rapport, "Determinants
of the Decision for Psychiatric Hospitalization," *Archives of General Psychiatry* 20 (March 1969), 321-328.

14. Thomas Scheff, *Being Mentally Ill* (Chicago, 1966), p. 105.

the examiner to comply with the legal requirement that
he testify to present insanity; the accused was caught, in
the medical view, in a process of inexorably unfolding
pathology.

Judicial deference toward medical opinion—even in
the early years of the century, when many doctors imagined judges to be an obstacle to expeditious treatment of
the insane—was a final factor that made the commitment of a detained individual more likely than his release. "The subject of insanity," explained one justice of
the Superior Court, "we all know is a special one, and
men of known ability in that special branch of the profession should determine these matters."[15] It was clearly
in the direct self-interest of the judge not to contradict
the findings of the examiners. To oppose their judgment
would not only slow down the operations of the court,
but would appear to constitute an unwarranted objection
to professional diagnosis and treatment. If the accused
were subsequently to harm himself or another person,
the judge would certainly be blamed. Only four times in
23 years—a period in which more than 15,000 persons
were examined—did a judge discharge a patient from the
Detention Hospital against the advice of the examiners.
Both judicial practices and medical traditions, therefore,
were heavily weighted in the direction of indefinite confinement. It is not surprising that once brought to the
Detention Hospital, eight in ten accused individuals were
committed.

But that raises the further question of why two out of
ten were not. Some accused individuals managed to convince the examiners that they did not require treatment.
An analysis of those cases illuminates the final stage of
the commitment process. They reveal that however deviant a person's reported behavior, an allegedly insane

15. Hon. Henry Melvin, "Proceedings in Commitment of the Insane," 5
Cal. St. Conf. Char. and Corr. 1909, p. 47.

individual who could manage to appear calm and rational in the presence of the examiner stood a fair chance of avoiding commitment. Brief records of the examinations that led not to commitment but to release from the Detention Hospital are available for the years 1910 to 1928—a period in which a total of 13,365 persons were examined and 2,740 (20.5 percent) were released.[16]

Those individuals released by the examiners were by no means all considered mentally healthy. Only 20 percent of those discharged were clearly considered to be "sane" and in need of no further treatment. Twelve percent were sent to a general hospital for medical treatment, and another 12 percent to a public or private relief home for extended care. The remaining 56 percent of those released were felt to be in clear need of further psychiatric treatment or observation: 25 percent were put into the custody of relatives who, "warned of the patient's condition, promised to obtain medical treatment and to look out for him." Six percent were released to friends on a similar basis. Ten percent were put on "probation" for periods ranging from one week to three months. Fifteen percent were released because relatives or friends promised to have them committed to a private mental hospital—an alternative that both examiners and judges were bound to applaud, since it would allow the accused to be confined and treated at no cost to the state. A few individuals were released after relatives requested that they be allowed to apply for voluntary admission to a state hospital.

The one-fifth of the discharged persons who were judged normal were those who, in the examiners' standard phrases, were "quiet and rational," "clear and ra-

16. *Records of Examination of Alleged Insane Persons and Orders of Discharge from Detention Hospital* (March 1909 to April 1929), 4 volumes, San Francisco City and County Records Center. Until 1919 the records contained only the names of the accuser and the accused. Beginning in 1920 the examiners also recorded the reason for the release.

tional," or "well-behaved and rational" while under observation. In several of these instances the examiners added important information about the social conflicts that had given rise to the accusation of insanity: "family quarrels a daily occurrence, divorce proceedings planned, but no sign of insanity"; "husband and wife incompatible"; "family row, husband advised to keep away from wife [the accused], as he often mistreated her"; "allowed to go with reprimand from judge to stop annoying her neighbors"; "released with understanding not to annoy husband and daughters"; "neighbors deny husband's claim that she is insane."

These cases reveal clearly that if the accused was capable of articulate and "reasonable" conversation with the examiner, and if the examiner could be made to see that a family or neighborhood dispute—not an individual's "illness"—was responsible for the accusation, the accused stood a chance of being released. If, on the other hand, the accused appeared afraid, perplexed, unhelpful, or disrespectful in the presence of the examiners, he would quite likely be judged insane and committed— although to the outside observer such behavior might seem quite rational under the circumstances. A case in point is that of an Austrian-born miner arrested for vagrancy in 1922 and brought to the Detention Hospital for examination. After noting that after several days in detention he felt "persecuted," the examiners recorded the only other behavior "indicating insanity": "he acts in a very surly manner toward the court interpreter who has interested himself in his welfare." Lack of gratitude for official kindness was the final demonstration of this individual's irrationality; the same day he was committed to the Napa State Hospital.

An additional finding of great interest concerns the sex of those accused of insanity but released by the examiners. Whereas 58 percent of those committed were men, 65 percent of those released were men. Though women made up 42 percent of those committed, they comprised only 35 percent of those discharged. Why were men more likely to be released? Did they perhaps more commonly possess the capacity to respond "clearly and rationally" to situations of great stress—particularly to male physicians legally empowered to detain them indefinitely? Or did the examiners perhaps assume, as the next chapter will suggest, that a woman accused of disturbed behavior was more likely to require institutional shelter or treatment? Whatever the reason, once a woman had entered the Detention Hospital, she was somewhat more likely than her male counterpart to be judged insane.

The decision for commitment depended, in sum, not only upon the recorded evaluation of the person's alleged insane behavior, but also upon his inability to appear "calm and rational" at the moment of examination. Those 12,150 San Franciscans committed to insane hospitals between 1906 and 1929 were persons who, for any number of reasons, were judged intolerable at home or in the community, and who, furthermore, could not or would not converse dispassionately with the examiner while detained—usually against their will.

5

The San Francisco Insane,
1906-1929:
A Social Portrait

Who were the San Francisco insane? What can be said about the social backgrounds of the 12,150 people declared insane and committed between May 1906 and May 1929? I have already noted that the insane were an extraordinarily heterogeneous group. It would therefore be impossible to grasp their typical characteristics by stringing together a long list of individual cases. An understanding of what types of persons were pronounced insane in San Francisco in the early twentieth century depends upon a statistical analysis of a large number of cases—in this case a systematic sample of 1,229 insane persons. Such an analysis can provide an understanding of the social characteristics exhibited by persons brought to court and committed for the reason that they were "so far disordered in mind as to endanger the health, person or property of [themselves] or of others."

State law required the medical examiners to obtain the answers to twenty questions relating to each person's social background. A different list of questions relating to medical history and reported or observed behavior—which will be considered in the next chapter—was even longer.[1] In some cases the examiners could not get answers they considered reliable; in a handful of instances they claimed they could get no reliable informa-

1. For a complete list of the questions, see the Appendix.

tion at all. But in the overwhelming majority of cases they received extensive information—whether from "witnesses" or from the accused himself—which they believed to be accurate.

The key variables for grasping the social identity of the San Francisco insane are nativity, occupation, family relationships, age, and sex. Those committed for insanity in San Francisco were very likely to be unmarried adult males; in addition, they were heavily blue-collar, and evenly split between the foreign-born and the native-born. When we compare the insane to the general population, however, a number of other fascinating patterns, as well as some further questions, emerge. The foreign-born, usually assumed by contemporaries and later historians alike to have contributed a disproportionate share of the insane, turn out to have been no more prone to insanity than the native-born. The blue-collar portion of the population, as well as the unmarried and the widowed, were heavily overrepresented in the insane population. Women, though not disproportionately numbered among the insane, seem nevertheless to have been committed for strikingly different reasons than insane men.

II

No conviction about insanity was more widely shared in late nineteenth- and early twentieth-century America than the belief underlying the federal deportation legislation of 1907 (which provided for the deportation of any immigrant found to be insane during the first three years of residence in the United States): immigrants were more likely to fall victim to insanity than the native-born. Anti-immigration polemicists were perhaps most responsible for the spread of this belief, but official bodies like the Immigration Commission organized by Congress in 1907, as well as respected medical authorities, also helped disseminate it. As Dr. Thomas Salmon, Medical Director of the National Committee for Mental Hygiene, declared in 1912, "There is one factor in the prevalence of insanity in this country which overshadows all others. That factor is immigration."[2]

The *San Francisco Call* made the same point in a 1903 editorial, which put most of the blame for California's image as "the land of lunatics" on "immigrants from the Old World." They "have already a tendency to dementia," the *Call* explained, "owing to the very fact of their removal from the land of their birth to one which must of necessity bring about a radical change in their mode of living and a consequent reaction on their mental economy."[3]

The idea was so deeply rooted that recent historians dealing with insanity have also tended to accept it without seeking further evidence. The San Francisco commitment records, as well as national Census Bureau data on insanity published in 1914, show, however, that the alleged link between immigration and insanity was in fact illusory. As one dissenting medical authority, the neurologist E. C. Spitzka, explained in a 1906 interview: the "common belief that the ranks of the insane in the United States are largely recruited by [*sic*] immigrants

2. Dr. Thomas W. Salmon, address to the Poughkeepsie Academy of Medicine, January 29, 1912. Typescript, Thomas W. Salmon Papers, American Foundation for Mental Hygiene, Payne-Whitney Clinic, New York Hospital, p. 1. For a fascinating description of the techniques used at Ellis Island to separate normal and insane immigrants, see Salmon, "The Diagnosis of Insanity in Immigrants," *Annual Report of the Public Health and Marine-Hospital Service* (Washington, D.C., 1906), pp. 271-278. Barbara M. Solomon, *Ancestors and Immigrants* (Cambridge, Mass., 1956), pp. 122-151, surveys the views of the anti-immigrationists. The findings of the Immigration Commission can be sampled in the 61st Congress, 3rd Session, *Abstracts of the Reports of the Immigration Commission*, vol. 2 (Washington, D.C., 1911), pp. 227-251.

3. "Insanity in California," Editorial, *San Francisco Call*, November 27, 1903, p. 6.

from abroad . . . is not the case. . . . We are quite capable
of manufacturing our own insane without charging them
to importations from abroad."[4]

Between 1900 and 1930, according to the decennial
census, an average of 31 percent of San Franciscans in
each census year were foreign-born. Among the insane,
48 percent were foreign-born—an initially startling disproportion. But the foreign-born population as a whole
was made up almost exclusively of adults, both in San
Francisco and the rest of the nation. In San Francisco
between 1900 and 1930, more than 90 percent of the
foreign-born were at least 20 years old, compared to
approximately 60 percent of the natives. In the United
States as a whole between 1900 and 1930, an average of
92 percent of the foreign-born, compared to 54 percent
of the native-born, were at least 20 years old.

Since insanity was in almost every instance an adult
phenomenon, foreigners should naturally be expected to
provide a much higher proportion. Furthermore, foreigners were substantially more likely to be men, and
men comprised almost 60 percent of the insane nationwide. In San Francisco, between 1900 and 1930, 60 per-

4. Hale, *Freud and the Americans*, p. 80: "By 1911 the foreign born
made up 29 percent of the population of New York State, yet provided
48.02 percent of first admissions to insane hospitals." Grob, *Mental Institutions in America*, pp. 120-121: "In 1850, for example, 534 patients were
immigrants . . . while there were only 121 native-born inmates [on New
York's Blackwell's Island]. These figures were disproportionate, when one
remembers that the foreign-born constituted less than half of the city's total
population." Rothman, *Discovery of the Asylum*, p. 283: "In the middle
decades of the nineteenth century the foreign-born occupied a disproportionate number of asylum places, comprising a far greater percentage of
inmates than their numbers in the general population." The Department of
Commerce, Bureau of the Census, *Insane and Feeble-Minded in Institutions,
1910* (Washington, D.C., 1910), p. 26, provided all the evidence needed to
show that the alleged "disproportion" was spurious. Spitzka's remarks are
contained in "Is Reform Sensationalism Responsible for the Apparent
Increase in Insanity in the United States?" *New York Times*, May 13, 1906,
pt. 3, p. 4.

cent of the foreigners were male, whereas men were only 50 percent of the native-born. Among the San Francisco insane the same percentages occur: 62 percent of foreigners were male, against 54 percent of natives. In sum, if we control for both age and sex, the rate of insanity was not decidedly greater in the case of the foreign-born. Of all those in San Francisco between 1900 and 1930 who were male and at least 21 years old, more than 42 percent were foreign-born; of the insane, 48 percent were foreigners. When we consider the additional fact that foreigners in general were much more likely to lack relatives in the city—of the foreign-born insane 58 percent had none the court could locate, against only 42 percent of the natives—the gap in insanity rates may disappear entirely. For it seems likely that disturbed individuals without relatives in the city would be more liable to come to the attention of the court.

Hence, we may conclude that the foreign-born were so numerous among the committed insane because they were overrepresented in those categories of characteristics that most commonly produced the insane: adult males without family in San Francisco.[5]

Nor were individual foreign-born nativity groups distinctly overrepresented among the insane. The Irish and Germans, who each made up an average of 5 percent of the city's population between 1900 and 1930, contributed

5. In 1898 the California State Commission in Lunacy made the interesting contention that "the percentage of insane is larger among those of foreign birth who do not talk English than among those who do, which may probably be accounted for on the ground that their ignorance of the English tongue tends to isolate those who do not speak it, and therefore makes their struggle for life harder and their mental depression greater." 1 *St. Comm. Lun.* 1899, p. 32. Ignorance of English not only "isolated" the foreign-born, but perhaps also made it more difficult, as Chapter Four suggested, for them to demonstrate their "rationality" to policemen, doctors, and judges. Unfortunately, the medical examiners did not ask for the birthplace of the parents of the accused. We are therefore unable to distinguish the native-born of foreign parents from the rest of the native-born.

8 and 7 percent respectively to the insane population.[6] But that slight disproportion can be explained by pointing to the age distribution of those two nationality groups. Both contained a higher proportion of older persons—especially, in the case of the Irish, of older women —than any other foreign nativity group. No other foreign-born nativity groups were even slightly overrepresented among the insane.

If the anti-immigration polemicists had been consistent, they would have moved to ban interstate migration as well, for native-born migrants had a substantially higher rate of commitments for insanity than native Californians. Fifty-two percent of the total insane population of San Francisco were native-born Americans; of these exactly one-half were born in California and one-half in other states. Yet in San Francisco's native-born population between 1910 and 1930, a full two-thirds were California-born. As Dr. Aaron Rosanoff, an authority on eugenics and later a California asylum physician, observed in 1915, a New York-born migrant was more than two-and-a-half times as likely to become insane as a native-born Californian.[7] Was that not convincing evidence that migrants were more prone to insanity? Such a conclusion is tantalizing, but mistaken. For the migrant population must surely have been composed of a significantly greater proportion of adults than the native-born. Unfortunately, the Census Bureau did not cross-tabulate state of birth, age, and city of residence. It may be that internal migration is related to insanity, as numerous recent studies have argued, but adequate data are not available for the early twentieth century.[8] But it is also

6. These are exact figures—not subject to sampling error—since they are derived from a tabulation of the nationalities of all persons committed between 1906 and 1928.

7. Dr. A. J. Rosanoff, "Some Neglected Phases of Immigration in Relation to Insanity," *American Journal of Insanity* 72 (July 1915), 50-51.

8. All that the commitment and Census records permit us to say with

quite possible that native-born migrants, like immigrants, were disproportionately liable to be committed
simply because they were overrepresented among adult
males living without family. A California-born adult male
without relatives may well have been equally liable to be
declared insane.

III

Among the California insane, wrote the State Commission in Lunacy in 1899, "the largest proportion is of
patients who come from laboring and working classes;
and the smallest from the business and professional
classes. This is true even when the relative ratios of these
classes in the general population is considered."[9] The
San Francisco commitment records fully support the
Commission's judgment that the insane were over-
whelmingly lower-class or lower-middle class—although
that conclusion rests almost exclusively upon an analysis
of occupations, which provide only a rough index of class
positions.[10] The medical examiners' and judges' questions about the educational background and financial

---

assurance about internal migration is that each geographical region of the
United States, excluding California, supplied the same proportion to the
insane population as to the native-born non-Californians in the city—the
leaders being the East North Central (one-fourth) and the Middle-Atlantic
(one-fifth). An excellent survey of recent literature on migration and
mental illness is Mildred B. Kantor, "Internal Migration and Mental Illness," in Stanley C. Plog and Robert B. Edgerton, eds., *Changing Perspectives in Mental Illness* (New York, 1969), pp. 364-394.

9. 1 *St. Comm. Lun.* 1899, p. 32.

10. Studies in the sociology of mental disorders have ordinarily relied on
occupational and educational data to measure class, since adequate information about wealth or property is rarely available. Such studies—of which the
most important is August B. Hollingshead and F. C. Redlich, *Social Class
and Mental Illness* (New York, 1958)—must therefore do without the kind
of information that is at once the most useful statistically, because of its
numerical character, and the most significant socially. We may ascertain
with much greater accuracy the relative class position of a "merchant,"
"builder," "engineer," or "editor" if we know not only that he finished

resources of the accused were not sufficiently detailed to provide useful data.[11]

The 1,229 sample members reported a total of more than 130 different occupations, of which "housewife" (20 percent), "laborer" (14 percent), "clerk" (3 percent), and "seaman" (3 percent) were the most common; 6 percent were reported to have no occupation, and in 5 percent of the cases the space in which occupation was to be entered was left blank (Table 7).

If we omit the housewives and those with no occupation (of whom 80 percent were women), we obtain

---

common school, but also the approximate dollar value of his real and personal property.

Social historians dealing with nineteenth- and early twentieth-century America have often had to rely upon occupational data alone—a risky endeavor, since it is enormously difficult to determine the relative status of occupations in a period of such rapid specialization and shifting classifications. Yet occupational level does provide a rough approximation of class position, one which we must employ in the absence of a superior alternative. In coding the occupations entered in the commitment records, I employed the scheme developed by Stephan Thernstrom, in which each individual occupation is assigned either to the high white-collar, low white-collar, or skilled, semiskilled, or unskilled blue-collar. Thernstrom, *The Other Bostonians: Poverty and Progress in the American Metropolis, 1880-1970* (Cambridge, Mass., 1973), pp. 289-292.

11. The examiners attempted to determine only if the accused fit into one of five educational levels: illiterate, reads a little, common school, academic, and collegiate. In 85 percent of the cases the accused claimed, or was said, to have reached the common school level—but it is impossible to judge whether he finished, or only began, common school.

State law required the judge to determine whether the person committed could pay $15 a month ($20 after 1920) to cover the cost of confinement, or if a relative could be found with the requisite funds. In three-quarters of the cases the judges entered the phrase "no funds"—though it is questionable how persistent they were in trying to uncover family resources. The attorney for the State Commission in Lunacy—whose job included the task of tracking down relatives unwilling, but required by law, to pay—repeatedly bewailed the judges' failure to hunt far enough. For example, "Report of Attorney," 8 *St. Comm. Lun.* 1912, p. 42, and 9 *St. Comm. Lun.* 1914, pp. 24-25.

the frequency distribution for "rankable" occupations (Table 8).

It is immediately apparent that three-quarters of the San Francisco insane came from blue-collar backgrounds, only one-fourth from the white-collar ranks, and less than one in twenty from the high white-collar category—made up of "professionals" ranging from physicians and attorneys to teachers. More than one-half, furthermore, were from the semiskilled and unskilled segments of the blue-collar group—segments which in terms of social status may have been further "below" the skilled workers than the skilled workers were below the low white rank. Almost one-third of the men were unskilled laborers.[12]

Table 7

OCCUPATIONAL DISTRIBUTION OF THE SAN FRANCISCO INSANE,
1906-1929

Occupational category		Percent
High white-collar	(n=37)	3.2
Low white-collar	(n=168)	14.6
Skilled blue-collar	(n=157)	13.6
Semi skilled blue-collar	(n=266)	23.1
Unskilled blue-collar	(n=210)	18.2
Housewives	(n=234)	20.3
No occupation	(n=79)	6.9
		99.9

12. It should not be assumed that women in semiskilled positions had "higher status" jobs than unskilled male laborers, since female "servants," "waitresses," and "housekeepers"—"service" positions that have traditionally been designated "semiskilled"—probably had an equally low social status. In fact, it is debatable even in the case of men whether all semiskilled jobs offered higher status than unskilled labor; an argument could be made for combining the two levels into a single "lower blue-collar" category.

Table 8

DISTRIBUTION OF THE RANKABLE OCCUPATIONS OF THE SAN FRANCISCO INSANE, 1906-1929

Occupational Level	Males		Females		Total	
High white-collar	(n=27)	4.1	(n=10)	5.4	(n=37)	4.4
Low white-collar	(n=133)	20.4	(n=35)	18.8	(n=168)	20.1
Skilled	(n=138)	21.2	(n=19)	10.2	(n=157)	18.7
Semi skilled	(n=151)	23.2	(n=115)	61.8	(n=266)	31.7
Unskilled	(n=203)	31.1	(n=7)	3.8	(n=210)	25.1
		100.0		100.0		100.0

Clearly, the insane population was skewed toward the lower occupational levels. But to what extent was the general population of San Francisco similarly skewed? Were the insane in fact representative of the rest of the city's residents? A hand tabulation of the occupational structure of the city in 1910—based on the Population Report of the Census Bureau (Table 9)—reveals that blue-collar workers were substantially overrepresented, and white-collar underrepresented, among the insane.[13]

Whereas 66 percent of the city's adult male workers and 54 percent of the city's adult female workers were blue-collar, 76 percent of both the insane men and the insane women were blue-collar. Most striking of all is the strong overrepresentation of unskilled laborers among the insane men; the unskilled supplied a proportion two-and-a-half times as great to the insane population as to the general population. It is also of considerable interest that the semiskilled men were underrepresented among the insane—significantly more underrepresented, in fact, than the skilled workers. It is not possible to determine with assurance why men employed at that level should have supplied a much smaller proportion. But it seems possible that disturbed individuals would be less likely to qualify for, or keep, "service" jobs—which comprised three-quarters of the semiskilled category—because those positions involved interpersonal

13. Thernstrom, *The Other Bostonians,* p. 50, provides a detailed discussion of this method of determining a city's occupational structure. The only modification I have made is to subtract from the calculation those employed persons aged 11 to 20; the resulting figures therefore refer to the adult population of the city in 1910—the population which supplied virtually all of the insane. The 1910 figures are adequate as a rough gauge for the 1906-1928 period, since as Thernstrom has shown for Boston, the white-collar percentage was increasing in these years in the general population. If these percentages are not precisely accurate, therefore, they err in underestimating the percentage of white-collar workers—which would make the insane population even less representative of the general population than it already appears to be.

Table 9

OCCUPATIONAL DISTRIBUTION OF THE SAN FRANCISCO INSANE
(1906-1929) AND OF THE ADULT POPULATION OF
SAN FRANCISCO (1910), BY SEX

Occupational level	Males		Females	
	Insane	*Adults*	*Insane*	*Adults*
High white-collar	4.1	3.1	5.4	5.3
Low white-collar	20.4	31.1	18.8	40.9
Skilled	21.2	19.1	10.2	5.2
Semi skilled	23.2	34.1	61.8	47.9
Unskilled	31.1	12.6	3.8	0.7
	100.0	100.0	100.0	100.0
Total white-collar	24.5	34.2	24.2	46.2
Total blue-collar	75.5	65.8	75.8	53.8
	100.0	100.0	100.0	100.0

relationships with clients in a more direct way than skilled or unskilled labor.

Among the female employed, low white-collar workers—engaged primarily in clerical and professional service—appear to have been extremely unlikely to be labeled insane. Women in those groups supplied more than twice as many individuals, proportionally, to the general work force as to the insane population. Although we must interpret the occupational spread of the female insane with caution—since it is based upon the 74 percent of women sample members who had a rankable occupation—the possible statistical error is not great enough to account for a disproportion of that size.

The commitment records clearly reveal that the San Francisco insane were heavily, and disproportionately, drawn from the blue-collar ranks. It might be objected that the commitment records were perhaps "biased" in favor of lower-class groups, since private mental hospitals did exist and since those from higher status backgrounds may have supplied a disproportionate share of the approximately 30 persons a year who after 1911 bypassed the court under the "voluntary admission" program. But those voluntary admissions never made up more than 5 percent of the total number admitted each year from San Francisco. Even if all 30 persons were white-collar—an unlikely proposition—the proportions of blue- and white-collar commitments would not be seriously affected. Similarly, the number of private mental hospital patients was too small to reduce materially the high disproportion of blue-collar commitments. In 1908 "private institutions licensed to care for mental cases" in all of northern California had a total capacity of only 245 beds; in 1928 they could accommodate only 435 patients. The four public state hospitals in northern California, on the other hand, had an actual patient population of 6,555 persons in 1908 and 9,300 persons in 1928. Private mental patients, therefore, could not have comprised any more than 4 percent of the mental patients in northern California; and it is unlikely that more than two-thirds of all the private hospital beds were filled.[14]

Furthermore, "higher status" patients and their families may have had some incentive to prefer the state hospital to private hospitals. Although state institutions

14. 6 *St. Comm. Lun.* 1908, pp. 105-107; 4 *Cal. Dept. Instits.* 1928, pp. 119, 139. A report in 5 *St. Comm. Lun.* 1906 stated that the five private, licensed sanitariums in northern California had 60 percent of their beds filled on September 1, 1906 (p. 119).

could not offer the same elegance of decor, patients with adequate funds could become "pay patients" at a rate of up to 40 dollars a month—compared to 15 dollars for regular patients and 100 dollars or more for private hospital patients—and thereby obtain superior accommodations, meals, and service. Superintendents encouraged this double standard of care since the additional money entered a contingency fund of which they could dispose as they saw fit.[15] In sum, therefore, it does not seem likely that the court commitment records were "biased" in such a way as to overestimate seriously the number of blue-collar individuals hospitalized for insanity.

IV

While the blue-collar population of San Francisco was heavily overrepresented among the insane, married persons were enormously underrepresented. The insane were much less likely to be married, and more likely to be early widows, than adults in the general population. Census figures for 1900, 1910, 1920, and 1930 give a precise measure of the difference. Whereas 36 percent of the insane were married, between 45 and 50 percent of San Franciscans over 15 years of age were married in each census year. Indeed, the real gap is considerably larger, since the insane population was almost com-

15. In 1899 the State Commission in Lunacy noted that "the hospitals have always made extra provision for pay patients, given them a somewhat more varied diet, and, where possible, better furnished rooms." The Commission recommended that the practice continue since it was the largest source of revenue for the contingency fund. 1 *St. Comm. Lun.* 1899, p. 19. The *San Francisco Call* reported the practice to be flourishing in 1912. "Receipts from Pay Patients Increase," January 20, 1912, p. 12. The San Francisco commitment records reveal that at least as late as 1914—when the sister of a sample member was reported by the judge to be willing to pay $40 per month for a private room—the practice was still in operation. But opposition to the double standard was growing. 6 *St. Bd. Char. and Corr.* 1915, pp. 180-182.

pletely (97 percent) over the age of 20, while an average of only 70 percent of San Franciscans in the four census years were over 20. If we recompute the census and commitment figures so that they include only those over 20, we find that 36 percent of the insane were married, whereas just under 60 percent of San Franciscans were married in all three decades.

The difference between the insane and the general population persists when we control for sex and age. Of women in San Francisco over 20 years of age, an average of 60 percent were married in the four census years; but of the insane women over 20, only 50 percent were married. Of the group aged 25 to 44, in which there are fewer widows, a constant 70 percent of San Francisco women were married, compared to 58 percent of the insane women. Of men in San Francisco, 50 percent between the ages of 25 and 44, and 60 percent of those above 44, were married; among the insane in the 25 to 44 age group, 24 percent were married, and in the over-44 age group, 37 percent were married. Census Bureau figures on the insane in the United States in 1910, moreover, disclose a pattern virtually identical to that of San Francisco.[16]

In addition, the insane were much more frequently early widows and widowers than the rest of the population. Among the insane women, one in five was already a widow in the 40 to 44-year-old age group, compared to one in ten in the general population. With men the same pattern occurs. In the group aged 50 to 59, 7 percent of San Francisco males were widowers; among the insane, 23 percent were widowers. In the older age groups, the general population and the insane population display comparable rates.

16. Bureau of the Census, *Insane and Feeble-Minded in Institutions, 1910*, p. 48. Figures for the general population of San Francisco were calculated from the *Population* volumes of the *Census of the United States* for 1900, 1910, 1920, and 1930.

Distinguishing the married and the widowed by both sex and nativity, the same tendency again stands out. Foreigners in San Francisco, male and female, were somewhat more likely to be both married and widowed than natives, as were the foreign insane. But the gap between the insane and general populations in rates of marriage and widowhood remain constant; the foreign insane were less often married and more often early widows and widowers than foreigners in general.

Commitment for insanity correlates therefore quite clearly with both the unmarried state and with early widowhood, but it is not a simple matter to explain the correlation. One might suspect that disturbed persons were less likely to seek or find willing mates, or even that marriage itself reduced a person's chances of suffering serious emotional problems. The Census Bureau's "expert special agent" on insanity confidently asserted in 1914 that "the large percentage of single persons among the insane is not to be interpreted as indicating that the single are more liable to become insane than the married. It means rather that the insane as compared with the normal are less likely to marry." This conclusion is certainly plausible, but not demonstrable; it does not seem impossible that marriage may have served in an urban, industrial society to reduce the pressures that promoted mental disorder or nervous tension.[17]

On the other hand, the most likely explanation would

17. Bureau of the Census, *Insane and Feeble-Minded in Institutions, 1900*, p. 48. Writing a generation earlier, the California Commissioner in Lunacy judged that "marriage is one of the most powerful agencies in preventing the increase of [insanity]. . . . The kindly and calming influences of the domestic circle, the greater regularity of habits, the freedom from inordinate passions and dissipated tendencies, all have their due effects in keeping the mind in a proper state of equilibrium, which is sanity." Dr. E. T. Wilkins, *Insanity and Insane Asylums* (Sacramento, 1872), p. 49. See also Benjamin Malzberg, *Social and Biological Aspects of Mental Disease* (Utica, 1940), p. 129: "It does not seem possible to rule out entirely the directly beneficial effects of matrimony, especially in the case of men."

seem to be that the married did exhibit an equal proportion of abnormal symptoms, but that family members preferred, or felt compelled, to tolerate such behavior—perhaps especially in the case of men. Those who came into contact with single disturbed persons—especially those with no family at all—probably had fewer scruples about sending them to the Superior Court for commitment.

In the case of early widows and widowers, it seems likely that the loss of one's spouse must have been so unsettling as to promote behavior which others perceived as disordered and requiring confinement. For the reverse situation is clearly implausible: married persons with mental or nervous problems could not for that reason have been any more likely to lose their spouses.[18] The medical examiners of the San Francisco Superior Court were certainly of this opinion; on numerous occasions they judged that "worry over loss of spouse" was the "cause" of insanity. In 1906 a recently widowed 57-year-old housewife was committed by her son. Since her husband's death she had been uncleanly and had failed to recognize her relatives; moreover, "there is a history of her having been consorting with several unknown men very recently." The root cause of her deviance was said to be "worry over loss of husband." One month later a judge committed a 26-year-old widow accused by her father of harboring religious delusions. Her belief that

18. Malzberg, *Social and Biological Aspects of Mental Disease*, p. 130, reaches the same conclusion. On the other hand, using data from the New York State Hospitals between 1929 and 1931, he shows that the insane were much more likely than the general population to be divorced—which suggests that marriages of individuals with mental or nervous problems were particularly unstable. In San Francisco, however, less than 5 percent of the insane were divorced, compared to 3 percent of adult men, and 5 percent of adult women, in the general population in 1930—the year in which the general divorce rate was the highest it had been in the twentieth century. In San Francisco, therefore, the insane were not disproportionately made up of divorcees.

"God has selected her to save the world" was traced to "loss of husband and disappointment in subsequent love affair."

The court physicians went considerably beyond the question of marital status in their investigation of family relationships. The examiners also attempted to determine which of his parents each accused person resembled most physically and mentally, and whether any of his relatives were or had been insane, alcoholic, nervous, eccentric, or otherwise defective. The hereditarian assumptions behind the latter question were quite consciously avowed; heredity was still assumed to be a predisposing cause of insanity in the vast majority of cases.[19] Evidence of insanity in an earlier generation seems to have been taken in many commitment hearings as ipso facto proof that any disturbed or disturbing behavior exhibited by the accused was grave enough to necessitate his confinement.

Why, one might ask, did the examiners care to inquire separately into the question of parental resemblance, when they had already investigated the matter of deviant or insane relatives, including parents? Did they perhaps assume that a woman who resembled her father, or a man his mother, were thereby to some degree abnormal? Such would seem to be a legitimate deduction.[20] Doubtless an accused person who resembled the "wrong" parent would not on that account alone be declared insane; but that fact might contribute one additional measure of proof that he needed treatment. It is of course possible,

19. Hale, *Freud and the Americans*, pp. 76-83; Charles E. Rosenberg, "The Bitter Fruit: Heredity, Disease, and Social Thought in Nineteenth Century America," *Perspectives in American History* 8 (1974) 189-235.

20. Rosenberg, "The Bitter Fruit," p. 196, notes that in the nineteenth century doctors commonly assumed that children inherited different attributes from each parent: from the mother temperament, internal viscera, stamina, vitality; from the father, intellect and external musculature. But according to that schema, every person would have both a mental and a physical relationship to each parent.

moreover, that some of the accused who claimed such a resemblance considered themselves deviant for that reason.

The court obtained responses to the question concerning parental resemblance in 80 percent of the cases. Of these, eight in ten were said to resemble the same parent both mentally and physically. The remaining 20 percent resembled both parents, one parent physically and the other mentally, or, in a handful of cases, neither parent.

Of those who resembled a single parent both mentally and physically—the only group with a sufficient number of cases for statistically meaningful results—the majority resembled the parent of the same sex. But if we control for sex, nativity, and religion, interesting differences emerge. Among both native-born and foreign-born Catholics, six in ten men and women resembled the parent of the same sex, with one group—the Italian men—topping 70 percent. Foreign-born Protestants matched the 60 percent figure of the Catholics, but native-born Protestants did not. Slightly more than half of native-born Protestant women (53 percent) resembled their fathers, and exactly one-half of the men claimed, or were reported to have, a likeness to their mothers. Either native-born Protestants among the accused were more frequently "abnormal" in this respect—an unlikely proposition—or else their culture placed less importance upon rigid sex role definition. It would appear that for Protestants born in America—heirs to a tradition which tended to promote individual opportunity and achievement, within certain bounds, even for women—it was more acceptable, both socially and psychologically, to claim a dominant resemblance to a parent of the opposite sex. Whether the medical examiners were themselves sensitive to such cultural differences it is impossible to ascertain. But the very fact that they investigated parental resemblance at all implies that they felt one form of resemblance was normal, another abnormal.

The examiners received considerably fewer affirmative responses when asking if the accused had any "eccentric," "chronically ill," or "insane" relatives. Only one-fourth of the accused claimed, or were believed by witnesses, to have such kin. Of these, almost 60 percent had "insane" relatives, over one-third had "alcoholic" relatives (9 percent had both insane and alcoholic kin), and 10 percent had nervous, peculiar, or eccentric relatives. A full three-quarters of all those with defective relatives were native-born—though only 52 percent of the insane population were natives. This initially surprising finding may be explained, however, by the fact that the native-born had more relatives in San Francisco in the first place. The examiners were no doubt able to discover more about them through local witnesses than they could about more distant relatives. But it may also be that the native-born, for cultural reasons, spoke more freely about mental or nervous problems in their families; they perhaps felt less stigmatized by such revelations. In addition, the foreign-born may have feared that disclosures about relatives might lead to their deportation, since, after 1907, any immigrant found to be insane during the first three years of residence in America could be forced to leave the country.

V

In her book *Women and Madness*, Phyllis Chesler makes the claim that "women of all classes and races constitute the majority of the psychiatrically involved population in America." Although her judgment may be questioned even for the 1960s and 1970s, it certainly does not hold true for San Francisco or the rest of the nation in the early years of the twentieth century, when "psychiatric involvement" signified, almost by definition, commitment to a state hospital.[21] Between 1900 and 1930, 45 percent

21. Phyllis Chesler, *Women and Madness* (New York, 1972), p. 333. Chesler's judgment—which applies to outpatient and in-patient cases in public and private hospitals—depends upon the unjustified exclusion from

of San Franciscans over the age of 20 were women; among the insane, 42 percent were women. In the United States as a whole, the pattern was similar though the female population was larger: 49 percent of Americans were women, but women accounted, in 1910, for 44 percent of the admissions to hospitals for the insane.[22] In San Francisco both native-born and foreign-born groups displayed the same difference. While a slightly smaller proportion of foreigners were women—four in ten— women made up 38 percent of the foreign-born insane. Of the native-born, 48 percent were women, compared to 46 percent of the native-born insane.

Yet even though women were not overrepresented among the insane, the commitment of women, and the medical and cultural assumptions underlying it, differed in a number of significant ways from the commitment of men. We have already seen that females were strongly underrepresented among those charged with insanity by doctors; they supplied a meager 20 percent of that group. That surprising finding, I have suggested, indicates not that women were any less likely than men to appeal to medical authorities, but that families, friends, or neighbors felt less need of medical sanction in support of their accusation. Moreover, once charged with insanity and held at the Detention Hospital, a female patient was more likely to be ordered committed. Only 35 percent of those discharged from the Detention Hospital after seeing the medical examiners were women. The underrepresentation of women among those accused initially by doctors

---

her tally of Veterans' Administration psychiatric patients, who are 98 percent male. Once those patients are included, the female majority disappears: men, who comprised 48.7 percent of the population of the United States in the 1960s, actually comprised a slightly higher 49.6 percent of all patients. See Chesler's Table 5, pp. 314-315, which provides the Veteran figures without incorporating them into her findings.

22. Bureau of the Census, *Insane and Feeble-Minded in Institutions, 1910*, p. 40.

and among those *not* committed after court examination seems to require a cultural explanation. It appears that both doctors and many other Americans had long assumed that women had a predisposition to certain types of sickness; like the aged, they could be expected to fall victim to and require treatment for any of a number of nervous or mental ills.

"Physicians assumed," writes Barbara Sicherman, "that women, whom they considered more emotional by nature and more subject to the vagaries of their reproductive systems, suffered even more acutely [than men] from the familiar burden of limited nervous resources and excessive strain." Moreover, their opinion may have been based on fact. "Because of numerous psychological and physical stresses on the Victorian woman, of which we still know too little," notes Regina Markell Morantz, "women were plagued with nervous exhaustion, or 'neurasthenia,' more often than men."[23]

23. Barbara Sicherman, "The Paradox of Prudence: Mental Health in the Gilded Age," *Journal of American History* 62 (March 1976), 898; Regina Markell Morantz, "The Perils of Feminist History," *Journal of Interdisciplinary History* 4 (Spring 1974), 652, n. 7. See also Carroll Smith-Rosenberg, "The Hysterical Woman: Sex Roles in Nineteenth Century America," *Social Research* 39 (Winter 1972), 652-678; Carroll Smith-Rosenberg and Charles Rosenberg, "The Female Animal: Medical and Biological Views of Woman and Her Role in Nineteenth-Century America," *Journal of American History* 60 (September 1973), 332-356; Barbara Ehrenreich and Deirdre English, *Complaints and Disorders: The Sexual Politics of Sickness* (Old Westbury, N.Y., 1973), pp. 15-44; John S. Haller, Jr., and Robin M. Haller, *The Physician and Sexuality in Victorian America* (Urbana, Ill., 1974), pp. 24-43; Donald Meyer, *The Positive Thinkers* (New York, 1965), pp. 46-59; Hale, *Freud and the Americans*, pp. 59-64, 232; Ann Douglas Wood, "'The Fashionable Diseases': Women's Complaints and Their Treatment in Nineteenth-Century America," *Journal of Interdisciplinary History* 4 (Summer 1973), 25-52; Gail Pat Parsons, "Equal Treatment for All: American Medical Remedies for Male Sexual Problems," *Journal of the History of Medicine and Allied Sciences* 32 (January 1977), 55-71. Parons's and Morantz's work is particularly useful in challenging the common charge, expressed most clearly in Wood's article, that Victorian male physicians harbored a distinctively hostile attitude, consciously or unconsciously, toward their female patients.

Whatever the relative susceptibility of the sexes to mental and nervous disorder, it is clear that many physicians—perhaps especially general practitioners like the medical examiners, who had little or no experience in neurology or psychological medicine—considered women more liable to succumb than men. Even the standard American treatise on insanity in the 1880s claimed that the male's "nervous system, though capable of greater endurance, is not so sensitive to delicate impressions" as the female's. Menstruation, often accompanied by "a variety of abnormal circumstances, such as headache, fever, nervous derangement," was "a fruitful source of the great variety of nervous and debilitated conditions which so many women of modern society suffer." Among women of the "upper classes," the treatise argued, "there is scarcely [one] . . . who is not more or less irregular in her menstrual discharges . . . from causes which are the result entirely of an artificial and abnormal mode of existence."[24]

"Hundreds of persons," trumpeted the *San Francisco Morning Call*'s editorialist in 1889, "chiefly women, and generally women of high culture and brilliant intellect, are now suffering tortures from what the doctors call nervous prostration. [It is] a disease, partly bodily and partly mental, which afflicts a large proportion of the most gifted women in the country, and is sending many of them to the asylums."[25]

It is true, as Barbara Ehrenreich and Deirdre English have stressed, that medical opinion on female susceptibility to nervous disorder often distinguished between laboring women and women of leisure—whose "artificial

24. Dr. William A. Hammond, *A Treatise on Insanity in Its Medical Relations* (New York, 1883), pp. 101, 105. At the time of the book's publication, Dr. Hammond was president of the American Neurological Association.

25. "Insanity in California," Editorial, *San Francisco Morning Call*, April 19, 1889, p. 4.

mode of existence," in Dr. Hammond's phrase, was responsible for such ills. Working women frequently appeared to be free of the psychic turmoil to which women seemed to be predisposed.[26] Is there any way to determine whether in the early years of the twentieth century the San Francisco medical examiners, or the relatives, friends, or neighbors of the insane, actually operated on the assumption that the female accused were so predisposed—given the fact that most of the women committed came from the blue-collar segment of the working class?[27]

There are a number of indications in the court commitment records that the accused women were indeed often viewed as particularly prone to mental or nervous disorder. One such piece of evidence consists of the responses to the examiners' question about the "duration of present attack." In 85 percent of the cases, the examiners were able to estimate how long the individual had been manifesting the current mental or nervous problem. Forty percent were undergoing attacks that had lasted one month or less; another 30 percent had suffered between one and six months, and 10 percent each fell into the six-month to two-year, two-year to four-year, and over four-year ranges. The duration figures were therefore heavily skewed in the direction of shorter attacks.

But controlling for sex, we discover that of those with the shortest attacks—seven days or less—70 percent were men. Women, on the other hand, had 54 percent of

26. Ehrenreich and English, *Complaints and Disorders*, pp. 11-14.

27. One-fourth of the women committed in San Francisco, it must be remembered, did not have an occupation that could be ranked: 20 percent were "housewives," and 6 percent had "no occupation." It is possible that these women were more "leisured" than those with rankable positions, but there is no way to be sure. We can safely state, however, that at least 60 percent of all women committed were members of the "blue-collar working class."

the attacks lasting more than two years and 56 percent of those over four years—a striking disproportion, since only 44 percent of those whose attacks could be measured were women. Women had attacks of longer duration than men in every nativity group and in every occupational group in which women were numerous enough to compute (low white-collar, semiskilled, housewives, and no occupation).

As we would expect, women also stood out among those with a history of previous commitments. Among the 20 percent of the sample members who had been previously committed, women made up 37 percent of those with only one previous commitment, but 55 percent of those with two, and 60 percent of those with three. Likewise, if we compute the total duration of previous commitments, women predominate among those with the most time spent in mental hospitals. Of those with a total duration of one year or less, two-thirds were men; but of those over one year, more than one-half were women, and of those over three years, 60 percent were female.[28]

Why should women have had attacks of longer duration than men? We might suspect that their relative age distribution could account for part of the difference, since men were overrepresented among those insane persons in their twenties—a group which, we might suppose,

28. On the other hand, published statewide figures show that women accounted for a disproportionately high number of "parolees" from state hospitals. Up to 1928, 55 percent of the 12,500 paroles from state hospitals were granted to women, although women comprised a minority of commitments. We must note, however, that a parole was not the same as a discharge; nor did it represent a "cure." It meant simply that a relative was willing to care for the individual for a period of weeks or months. It is not surprising that relatives should have been more willing to care temporarily for female insane persons, who would probably appear to be easier to "control." Hospital superintendents would probably for the same reason have had fewer scruples about granting parole to female patients than to male patients. (Parole figures calculated from biennial reports of the State Commission in Lunacy and the State Department of Institutions.)

would have shorter attacks than older people. But in fact men between 20 and 29 were just as likely to have long attacks as men in every other age range, with the single exception of men in their seventies.

The fact that women had relatives in San Francisco with greater frequency can explain part of this difference. For those with relatives were more likely to have had longer attacks prior to commitment—doubtless because those living with or near relatives were tolerated longer than those who came into contact only with neighbors, landlords, employers, police, and doctors. Of those brought to court on an affidavit signed by police, for example, 40 percent had attacks lasting seven days or less, compared to 12 percent of those brought to court by relatives.[29]

But the presence of relatives is not sufficient in itself to account for the disproportion. Even when we control for relatives, women continue to stand out. Of those sample members with relatives in the city and attacks lasting more than two years, women were almost six in ten. Yet women were still a disproportionate one-half of those with long attacks and no relatives. The preponderance of women among those with the longest attacks prior to commitment can best be explained, it seems, by assuming that the examiners, witnesses, and perhaps the women themselves believed that females had a predisposition to fall victim to—and need treatment for—mental or nervous disturbances.

Another piece of evidence in the commitment records points to the same conclusion. In the first place, among those sample members said to have had insane or deviant relatives, more than 50 percent were women, al-

29. This hypothesis is supported by Egon Bittner's recent finding that the police are much less likely to conduct a suspected mentally ill person to the psychiatric hospital if they determine that he has relatives in the area. Bittner, "Police Discretion in Emergency Apprehension of Mentally Ill Persons," *Social Problems* 14 (Winter 1967), 278-292.

though only 42 percent of the insane population was female. This initially surprising figure can be explained by the fact that three-quarters of the insane women had relatives in the city compared to only one-half of the men. Having relatives so much more often, the women would be expected to have a larger proportion of those considered defective.

But a second pattern cannot be explained so readily. Six in ten of those whose relatives were said to be "insane" were women, while women made up only four in ten of those with "alcoholic" relatives. Of course, the alleged alcoholics among the insane were predominantly men, and they might have admitted more easily to having alcoholic relatives than the women; or the medical examiners may have pressed them harder than they did nonalcoholics, in an effort to trace their habit into a previous generation. But the striking disproportion of women among those with "insane" relatives cannot be explained in a similar fashion, since women were a distinct minority among those charged with insanity. The only possible conclusion, it would seem, is that women were either more liable than men to admit to having disturbed relatives, or that examiners—and perhaps the women themselves—believed with greater frequency that they in fact had insane relatives. In either case, we confront what must have been the common assumption that women possessed a weak nervous constitution and were particularly susceptible to breakdowns. A woman accused of insanity might for that reason be more liable to perceive such weakness in the rest of her family and be more willing to admit it. The examiners, furthermore, may have pressed harder for such evidence when interrogating female detainees, believing that women were either more likely to detect, or agree to reveal, a history of familial insanity.

A final piece of evidence in support of the view that women were considered to have a special need for psychiatric confinement is the disproportionate number of females accused in the over-65 age group. Whereas an average of one in sixteen San Francisco women was over 65 from 1900 to 1930, one in ten insane women was over 65. Insane men over 65 were slightly more frequent than "normal" men in the same age group, but the difference was not statistically significant.

How can we account for the disproportionate commitment of aged women? The explanation lies, it would seem, in a combination of cultural assumptions and institutional realities. Aged women with symptoms of senility or other disorders may have been considered insane more frequently because women in general were thought more likely to suffer mental and nervous afflictions. Or perhaps aged women without funds for retirement seemed to be particularly in need of a permanent "home" in which they could be sheltered. For men, no doubt, it was more acceptable both socially and psychologically to take to the streets, relying for survival on soup kitchens and other handouts.

But why should a desire to provide permanent shelter for aged women have involved the state hospital for the insane instead of the municipal almshouse? Statistics on admissions to San Francisco's Relief Hospital for the Aged and Infirm—as the almshouse was called after 1910—provide part of the answer. In San Francisco, as in the rest of the country, municipal almshouses in the late nineteenth and early twentieth centuries were rapidly becoming specialized institutions for the care of aged and destitute males. At the turn of the century, eight in ten of those admitted in San Francisco were men, and in 1910 —and thereafter—the figure was nine in ten. Before 1910 those in their sixties were the most numerous of any ten-year age group. Starting in 1911, and constantly thereafter, those in their seventies were the largest group.[30]

30. "Annual Report of the Health Department of the City and County of

The Census Bureau likewise demonstrated in its nationwide studies of "paupers in almshouses" in 1904 and 1910 that almshouses were increasingly restricted to the aged and were becoming "more and more given over to the care of destitute men." Yet until 1927, when the Laguna Honda Home was opened by the city, no other public institution existed in San Francisco to shelter destitute aged women. Moreover, San Francisco—unlike most California counties—provided no "outdoor" relief for the aged poor until 1929. Since aged women could not take to the streets in a socially acceptable manner— as even many of the male residents of the almshouse did during the spring and summer—there was no alternative to the state hospital for those females who were either no longer welcome among their relatives or who no longer had a home.[31]

It was a simple matter, furthermore, to demonstrate that almost any aged person was insane, since senility was increasingly equated with old age, and "senile psychosis" was scarcely distinguishable from senility itself. As early as 1877 a state hospital superintendent, outraged by the common practice of committing harmless old persons to his institution, declared that "cases of purely senile dementia . . . should not properly be numbered among the insane." His protest suggests that the practice of confining homeless old people was well established in the nineteenth century. Yet psychiatric theory in the early twentieth century defined "senile dementia"

San Francisco," in San Francisco Board of Supervisors, *San Francisco Municipal Reports* (San Francisco), annual.

31. Department of Commerce, Bureau of the Census, *Paupers in Almshouses, 1910* (Washington, D.C., 1915), p. 19; San Francisco Grand Jury, *Preliminary Report of the Grand Jury, April 19, 1928* (San Francisco, 1928), p. 18; Heller Committee for Research in Social Economics of the University of California, *The Dependent Aged in San Francisco* (Berkeley, 1928), pp. 2, 10, 17; *First Biennial Report of the State Department of Social Welfare* (Sacramento, 1929), pp. 164, 177, 181.

as, in the German psychiatrist Emil Kraepelin's formulation, "a morbid exaggeration of the changes seen in normal senility"—and as a morbid condition it required "treatment."[32]

Almost any personality quirk in an aged person was taken as evidence of senility. Suspiciousness, failure of memory, or slowed reflexes were signs of deterioration; if individuals displaying those signs became bothersome, then the deterioration could easily be judged "morbid."[33] Underlying this near equation of "normal" and "abnormal" senility was the basic cultural assumption that old age itself was in essence a degenerative process—a cultural viewpoint that may have emerged in the nineteenth century when old people appeared to be losing their functional role in an urbanizing society.[34] But in San Francisco, for institutional and perhaps cultural reasons, "senility" appears to have become "insanity" more

32. Dr. E. T. Wilkins, "Resident Physician's Report," *Report of the Board of Trustees of the Napa State Asylum for the Insane* (Sacramento, 1877), p. 23; Emil Kraepelin, *Lectures on Clinical Psychiatry*, 3rd Eng. ed. trans. Thomas Johnstone (London, 1913), p. 230. Kraepelin's method of psychiatric classification was "accepted orthodoxy" in the United States from the late 1890s to the late 1920s. Hale, *Freud and the Americans*, p. 84.

33. Dr. Aaron Rosanoff, a California State Commissioner in Lunacy, provided a full list of "indications" of senile dementia in his *Manual of Psychiatry*, 6th rev. ed. (New York, 1927), pp. 236-237. He vacillated about whether to call those indications normal or abnormal components of the aging process. In his work of 1895, *The Rules of Sociological Method* (New York, 1938), p. 51, Emile Durkheim attacked the commonplace equation of old age and morbidity: "If old age is already synonymous with morbidity, how distinguish the healthy from the diseased old person?"

34. David Hackett Fischer, *Growing Old in America* (New York, 1977), especially pp. 127-132; H. Warren Dunham, "Sociological Aspects of Mental Disorders in Later Life," in Oscar J. Kaplan, ed., *Mental Disorders in Later Life*, 2nd ed. (Stanford, 1956), pp. 157-177; George Rosen, "Psychopathology of Aging: Cross-Cultural and Historical Perspectives," in *Madness and Society: Chapters in the Historical Sociology of Mental Illness* (New York, 1968), pp. 229-246. For the story of one San Francisco psychologist's efforts to "rehabilitate old age" through an "old age clinic" in the 1920s, see Lillien J. Martin, *Salvaging Old Age* (New York, 1930).

frequently for aged women than for aged men. Typical of dozens of others was an 81-year-old woman who in 1918 was committed for the simple reason that she "cannot be cared for any longer at home." Unable to provide any "facts indicating insanity," the examiners managed to discover one piece of information to justify the committal: the duration of her "present attack," they reported, was "40 years."

6

"So Far Disordered in Mind":
The Intolerable Deviance
of the Insane

In 1908 the San Francisco police arrested a 34-year-old Swiss-born dairyman because, as the police reported to the court physician, he "goes up to strangers insisting on shaking hands because they are brothers." The doctor observed only that while confined at the Detention Hospital the man "spoke exclusively on religious subjects." The next day a judge ordered him committed to the Stockton State Hospital.

A 37-year-old unmarried woman, born in San Francisco, was brought to the Detention Hospital in 1914 upon an affidavit signed by her sister. Although she was "quiet and friendly" while in detention, her sister persuaded the examiner that she needed treatment. For "at age 18 she began to act silly, lost interest in all things which interest women, could no longer crochet correctly as formerly, takes no interest in anything at present." Those facts convinced the judge to commit her, the following day, to the Mendocino State Hospital.

In 1920 an Italian-born San Franciscan swore in an official affidavit that his 64-year-old wife was "peculiar, retiring, not industrious," and that, furthermore, she had been "hearing voices" for the last 23 years. A week later a mother brought her 16-year-old son, a schoolboy, to the hospital. She informed the examiner that her son "won't put shoes or stockings on, masturbates openly, won't go to school, is uncleanly." In each case no other facts were adduced in court to establish the person's insanity. Each of the accused individuals spent two days in detention and was then committed to a state hospital by a Superior Court judge.

None of the above cases was unusual; dozens more of each type—and of other types—could be cited from the court records of those San Franciscans declared insane between 1906 and 1929. But these examples are sufficient to remind us that the insane comprised a motley assortment of deviants, some of whom were doubtless "mentally ill" and incapable of caring for themselves, but others of whom appear from the record not to have been mentally ill even when that elastic category is stretched to the limit. As California hospital superintendents had complained since the mid-nineteenth century, deviant but apparently sane individuals made up a large proportion of their hospital admissions. State law provided local communities with a handy means of ridding themselves of undesirable charges; state law also forced families financially burdened with a disturbed or disturbing relative to seek commitment, since subsidies for family or community care were nonexistent.

The San Francisco commitment records allow us to try to estimate what proportion of the insane exhibited clear symptoms of mental disability and what proportion did not. To seek such an estimate is risky at best, since the records provide only the medical examiner's account of the allegedly insane person's behavior. Even when the records indicate no clear mental disturbance, it is possible that the individual was in fact seriously disturbed; likewise, when the medical examiner, on the basis of a brief encounter with the accused, offered a diagnosis of, for example, "dementia praecox," it is quite possible that the individual was in fact sane.

The basic point to underline is that the examiners, relying on second-hand information about persons whom they did not know, and examining them only perfunctorily in prison-like conditions, were themselves incapable of judging the true severity of the symptoms. Apparent symptoms of "disease" might in fact be responses to detention itself. The examiners could ordinarily respond to the accused only as an abstract case of reported characteristics and as a detainee in involuntary confinement, not as a concrete human being whose everyday behavior derived meaning from a social and familial context. As one Oakland Superior Court judge candidly acknowledged in 1908, "People improperly charged with insanity come into court so nervous that they appear insane."[1]

Some reported behavior does indicate the strong possibility of a severe disturbance. But from the relatively infrequent appearance of such behavior in the records, we may suppose that only a minority of the accused were "so far disordered in mind" as to endanger themselves or others—the legal criteria for commitment. The fact that severe symptoms were sometimes reported would seem in itself to constitute evidence that when they were not reported, they were probably absent.

The examiners recommended commitment generally after recording instances only of behavior—actions, habits, perceptions, or beliefs—which seemed to them inappropriate, peculiar, deviant. They did not in general claim that the behavior of the accused interfered with his adequate functioning or represented a threat to himself or anyone else—although it is clear that in some cases the examiners felt the accused to be a threat to established canons of morality. Commitment proceedings were initiated in most cases not because the behavior of

1. Hon. Henry Melvin, "Proceedings in Commitment of the Insane," 5 *Cal. St. Conf. Char. and Corr.* 1909, p. 47. An earlier version of this chapter was published as "The Intolerable Deviance of the Insane: Civil Commitment in San Francisco, 1906-1929," *American Journal of Legal History* 20 (April 1976), 136-154.

the accused revealed either grave disability or destructiveness, but because relatives, doctors, police, or neighbors decided they could no longer tolerate his or her deviant behavior.

Dr. Alan A. Stone, a leading authority on law and psychiatry, has recently noted that the "convenience function" of civil commitment—the use of the commitment statute to relieve society or the family "of the trouble of accommodating persons who, though not dangerous, are bothersome"—has "seldom been explicitly acknowledged . . . although at some points during the past century it has been the only goal actually achieved. . . . It is, therefore, a typical instance of the clandestine decision making role of mental health practitioners which allows society to do what it does not want to admit to doing, i.e., confining unwanted persons cheaply." The San Francisco commitment records offer firm evidence that the convenience function was paramount in California in the first third of this century.[2]

II

In completing the commitment form, the examiners recorded in each case, under the heading "facts indicating insanity," one or more of the alleged insane person's traits, habits, actions, perceptions, or beliefs. In almost all cases the record included behavior reported by witnesses, and in three-fourths of the cases the examiners also noted what they themselves, or a Detention Hospital attendant, had observed. Interestingly, ten sample members (just under 1 percent) were committed without any entry whatsoever under "facts indicating insanity." Of these ten, seven were over the age of 65; of the remaining three, one was a former mental patient, and one had an insane mother. Although the number of cases is small, these figures tend to reinforce the argument in

2. Alan A. Stone, *Mental Health and Law: A System in Transition* (Rockville, Md., 1975), pp. 45-46.

Chapter Five that old people could sometimes be committed solely on the grounds of age.

The examiners gave no reason for their failure to record their own observations in one-fourth of the cases. It may be significant, however, that whereas almost 40 percent of all accused persons reportedly lacked relatives in San Francisco, only one-fourth of those about whom the examiners made observations had no kin in the city. Perhaps the presence of relatives put pressure on the examiners to do a more complete job.

Of the accused with "reported" behavior "indicating insanity," two-thirds had at least two distinguishable instances of such behavior, and one-third had at least three.[3] In Table 10 the most commonly mentioned behavioral characteristics are ranked in order of frequency.

Only six of these most common behavioral characteristics appear to suggest in themselves the clear possibility that the accused was suffering from a severe disability: "syphilis," "confused," "incoherent," "convulsions," "wanders aimlessly," and "loss of memory."[4] In

3. The records indicate that only a handful of the accused had more than three instances of reported behavior or more than two instances of observed behavior. In coding their behavior for computer analysis, therefore, I permitted each individual to have three of the former and two of the latter. In the few cases with more recorded behavior, I coded the first three instances of reported behavior and the first two instances of observed behavior. In the records as a whole, 99 different types of reported behavior could be distinguished, and 74 varieties of observed behavior. The behavioral data were put into machine-readable format in their original form, without "collapsing" them into broader categories. In subsequent manipulations of the data by the computer I did employ such categories.

4. Alcoholism is today commonly regarded as a seriously disabling "disease," but such does not appear to have been the case in the early twentieth century. Physicians did hold that "the long continued use of alcohol [brings] a change in the nutrition of the brain cells that renders entire restoration impossible," but most cases of "excessive alcohol" were viewed as bad habits, similar to masturbation. F. W. Hatch, "Operations under the Inebriety Law," 10 *St. Comm. Lun.* 1916, p. 16. For a critique of

the case of "syphilis," "convulsions," and "loss of memory," which most clearly imply disabilities stemming from physiological causes, the examiners only infrequently indicated a connection between underlying diseases and the detainee's disturbance. In only 14 of the 83 cases of syphilis did the examiners proceed to diagnose "general paralysis of the insane," an organic brain syndrome known to result from some cases of syphilis. In only 6 of the 39 cases of "loss of memory" did they actually diagnose "senile dementia." And never did they explicitly diagnose "epileptic insanity" in a patient with convulsions. It is clear that these individuals—especially those with syphilis and convulsions—were ill, but far from clear, to judge from the record, that they were mentally ill.

Once again, it is impossible to judge the severity of an individual's symptoms by reference to abstract behavioral characteristics. Doubtless some of the "depressed," "noisy," or "vile" were severely disturbed, and certainly some of the "confused" or "incoherent" were only mildly disordered. Moreover, some syphilitics were simply persons alleged to have had syphilis in the past, and who displayed no current infection, symptoms of general paralysis, or other forms of disturbance. Yet the terms the medical examiners commonly chose to describe the behavior of the accused appear to support the inference that their behavior was not on the whole severely disabling.

Furthermore, only two of the characteristics— "violent, dangerous," and "suicidal"—clearly implied that the accused was "dangerous to be at large," a fact to which

---

the contemporary view, see Craig MacAndrew, "On the Notion that Certain Persons Who Are Given to Frequent Drunkenness Suffer from a Disease Called Alcoholism," in Stanley C. Plog and Robert B. Edgerton, eds., *Changing Perspectives in Mental Illness* (New York, 1969), pp. 483-501. It was not until after World War II, according to MacAndrew, that the "new approach"—alcoholism as a "disease"—took hold.

Table 10

MOST COMMONLY REPORTED BEHAVIOR "INDICATING INSANITY,"
1906-1929

Reported behavior	Times reported	As percent of all reported behavior
Excessive alcohol	(165)	7.0
People "harming" him or her	(134)	5.7
Masturbation	(119)	5.0
Abnormally religious	(109)	4.6
Hears voices	(108)	4.6
Depressed	(91)	3.8
Syphilis	(83)	3.5
Confused	(72)	3.0
Incoherent	(63)	2.7
Threatened family member	(59)	2.5
Noisy	(58)	2.4
Vile language	(55)	2.3
Convulsions	(52)	2.2
Wanders aimlessly	(51)	2.2
Threatened neighbors	(48)	2.0
Violent, dangerous	(47)	2.0
Peculiar, queer	(43)	1.8
Sexual excesses	(43)	1.8
Loss of memory	(39)	1.6
Threatened official personnel	(39)	1.6
Nervous	(37)	1.5
Suicidal	(37)	1.5
		65.3

the examiner was legally required to attest. Even if we assume that all those who were alleged to have issued threats against family members, neighbors, or official personnel (policemen, doctors, nurses, relief home employees, Detention Hospital attendants) were in fact dangerous, "violent" characteristics would still comprise less than 10 percent of the total "facts indicating insanity."[5]

The great majority of the reported behavioral data establish only that, in the eyes of the examiners, the actions, beliefs, perceptions, or habits of the accused were inappropriate, troubling, or peculiar. In some cases, furthermore, they were plainly believed to be immoral as well. "Masturbation," "vile language," "sexual excesses," and to some degree "excessive alcohol" were characteristics that indicated a violation of explicitly articulated cultural norms. In these cases the examiners were acting not only as diagnosticians of "insane" behavior—behavior assumed to be out of touch with reality—but as guardians of civilized morality.

We can try to obtain a more complete picture of the proportion of merely deviant behavior, and of the clearly disabling or destructive behavior, by assigning each of the 99 distinguishable characteristics to one of seven categories, which are ranked in order of frequency:

1. Inappropriate and Immoral Personal Habits (26 percent): including primarily drug abuse, excessive alcohol, masturbation, sexual excesses, vile language, exhibitionism, uncleanliness, vagrancy, prostitution, accosting strangers, and throwing away money or property.

2. Irrational Beliefs, Fears, Perceptions (21 percent):

5. Recent studies tend to support the view that the incidence of violent or criminal behavior among former mental patients is lower than in the general population. The only exception to this pattern is the suicide rate. Scheff, *Being Mentally Ill*, p. 72; J. R. Rappeport, ed., *The Clinical Evaluation of the Dangerousness of the Mentally Ill* (Springfield, Ill., 1967), pp. 72-80; Kent S. Miller, *Managing Madness* (New York, 1976), ch. 4.

including chiefly delusions of persecution or grandeur, auditory or visual hallucinations, and fears of poison and electricity.

3. Organic Disability or Affliction, or Functional Incapacity (20 percent): including primarily syphilis, convulsions, loss of memory, inability to care for self, confusion, incoherence, ignorance of surroundings, failure to recognize relatives, and sitting in a fixed position.

4. Miscellaneous, Possibly Disabling, Functional Disturbances (11 percent): including such actions as aimless wandering, talking to self, refusing to eat, crying unnecessarily, refusing to talk, and "suicidal" inclination.

5. Threat to People or Property (9 percent): including violent, dangerous, or uncontrollable behavior, threats to family members, neighbors, or official personnel, and destruction of personal or public property.

6. Nervous or Depressive Symptoms (7 percent): including "nervous," "excitable," "restless," "depressed," and "worried."

7. Religious Delusions (6 percent): including "abnormally religious," "continually praying," and "visions of the devil."

It is clear from the frequencies of these "collapsed" categories that a full one-quarter of the behavior cited by the examiners under "facts indicating insanity" was actually "immoral" behavior—the nonobservance of well-articulated canons of morality. Another 20 percent of the characteristics were irrational beliefs; together with the religious delusions they comprised another one-quarter of the behavior. Another 9 percent were in the area of "threats," and 7 percent were nervous or depressive symptoms. Significantly, more than one-third of the "violent" behavior contained in the category of threats was directed against official personnel: policemen, doctors, nurses, and others. Such violence may in some cases have been less a symptom of disability than a response to detention.

Only 20 percent of the characteristics clearly indicated a serious disability, and only 11 percent suggested the clear possibility of an incapacitating disturbance. But these figures do not signify that 20 percent of accused individuals had such a disability, or that 11 percent may have been disabled, for the figures apply to the total of discrete behavioral characteristics, not to individuals. Some individuals with syphilis, for example, were also reported to be "incoherent"; some "aimless wanderers" also talked to themselves.

When we focus on individuals, therefore, these proportions decrease. Only 10 percent of the accused were clearly reported to have a serious disability, and only 5 percent had a potentially disabling disturbance. In addition, 5 percent reportedly threatened another person, and 11 percent were reportedly "violent"—but of these more than one-third were violent only after being detained in a public institution, usually the Detention Hospital itself.

Likewise, the fact that one-fourth of the total behavioral characteristics referred to immoral behavior does not signify that 25 percent of the insane were simply deviants—such as alcoholics, drug addicts, or vagrants—who exhibited only that single behavioral pattern. Some alcoholics were also exhibitionists; some vagrants masturbated; most "immoral" deviants displayed at least an irrational belief or a nervous symptom. When we look at individuals, therefore, we find that 7 percent of the alleged insane were accused *only* of immoral behavior. In those cases no other symptoms were reported. These addicts, alcoholics, vagrants, and prostitutes were usually brought to the hospital by the police—in several cases for the explicitly stated reason that the individual had been "bothering" public officials for some time.

As the medical examiner put it in committing Nina H., a 48-year-old pianist in 1922, "she has been irresponsible for years; has been a source of great annoyance to many institutions such as Y.W.C.A. Association, churches, etc.; recently arrested for vagrancy." The patient displayed no other symptoms whatsoever; in the Detention Hospital the examiner observed only that she was "quiet and good." In some cases the deviance of an individual appears to have consisted solely in his habit of pestering officials. In 1915 a 40-year-old clerk was put in detention on the grounds that "for three weeks he has been annoying the City Registrar, calling every day and insisting that he is a Deputy. Acted in a threatening manner toward City officials, said he would send everyone else to the Asylum." Noting that his illness was of "rapid onset," and that his "present attack" began "three weeks ago," the examiner had him committed to Napa State Hospital. In 1927, a Spanish laborer was committed after the Spanish consul signed an affidavit alleging simply that beginning two day earlier, he "called Spanish consulate and has annoyed them with nonsensical talk over international politics, writes letters to Queen of Spain and others."

Scores of case records support the judgment that the deviants were often committed simply on the report of immoral behavior. In 1922 a 36-year-old Mexican-born woman was brought to the Detention Hospital on the affidavit signed by her social worker, who alleged that she had "led an immoral life for several years past, although mother of three small children." The accused claimed that the Associated Charities Bureau was "persecuting her." Those "delusions of persecution," characteristically, were taken as further evidence of her need for detention and treatment.

In another case the same year, a 23-year-old Rumanian-born Jewish divorcée was accused by her neighbor of being "lazy, slovenly, careless of personal appearance, stays away from home for days, neglecting self and consorting with men." As if to acknowledge that the evidence indicating insanity was flimsy, the examiner added one final fact revealed by the neighbor: "in her youth," though not at present, "she was feeble-minded." In 1927, a 41-year-old Jewish widow, who had been detained one year earlier and then released, was again brought to the Detention Hospital. She had failed to keep up the anti-syphilitic treatment upon which her earlier release had depended. Moreover, as her sister reported to the examiner, she "has been very immoral of late."

In describing the behavior especially, though not exclusively, of "immoral" individuals, the examiners frequently, though perhaps unconsciously, used vivid rhetorical devices that portrayed the accused as wild, beastly, or spooky. In 1914 a 40-year-old woman was "arrested by police who found her on street driving horse at breakneck speed, *hair streaming*." Once in custody, "she asked the officer to have sexual relations with her at police station." A woman who had been in jail before coming to the Detention Hospital was said to have "*prowled* about at all hours of the night" while in the jail. A man with "religious delusions" was reported to have "*haunted* the churches praying a great deal." Another man, "ugly" and refusing to answer questions while in detention, "showed *superhuman* strength by breaking hospital bedstead with his hands." A male patient committed on the sole grounds of being a "pathological liar" also had an "erotic, *cunning* laugh." A "quarrelsome, irritable" detainee, similarly, was commited simply on the grounds that he was "erotic and seems to be *sex mad*." (All italics added.)

It is clear that many more women than men in the sample were committed on the sole grounds of sexual promiscuity—although the number of cases is too small to permit the inference that the same was true of the whole insane population. Male sample members were committed for such offenses as masturbation, homosexuality, "obscene history of syphilis," and "crime against nature" (sodomy), but never for "consorting with unknown" members of the opposite sex—as women frequently were. Such promiscuous behavior, as we would expect, may have been considered normal for men, but deviant for women.

One-third of the "immoral" deviants, it should be added, were former mental patients. While their reported behavior indicated no mental disturbance, the fact that they had been previously hospitalized was undoubtedly taken as evidence that their present deviant behavior was at its root a manifestation of mental illness. Unfortunately, it is not possible to determine whether their previous hospitalization was also based simply on reportedly immoral behavior. But the fact that two-thirds of the immoral deviants in the sample had not been treated previously suggests that, as a general rule, such deviants were originally confined on the grounds of immoral behavior, not because of a mental condition.

Table 11 gives the distribution of individuals in the sample according to their reported behavioral characteristics, and reveals the proportions of the disabled, the dangerous, the odd or peculiar, and the immoral among the San Francisco insane. The characteristics are ranked in such a way that any individual exhibiting more than one type of behavior is automatically placed in the "highest" applicable category. For example, an insane person with both a "clear disability" and "excessive alcohol" is ranked in the first category, an individual with both "violent" behavior and delusions is put in the category "violent actions," a person with both delusions and "immoral" behavior is placed in the "odd or peculiar" category, and a person exhibiting only immoral behavior is put in the category of "immoral" behavior. This ranking favors, therefore, the higher or more "serious" categories; it ensures that those persons classed as odd, peculiar, or immoral were not also reported to be either seriously disabled or violent. The table is purposely

Table 11

DISTRIBUTION OF BEHAVIOR "INDICATING INSANITY" AMONG
COMMITTED INDIVIDUALS, 1906-1929

Reported behavior		Percent
Clear disability	(n=122)	9.9
Possible disability	(n=60)	4.9
Violent actions (including while in detention)	(n=134)	10.9
Threats to others (including while in detention)	(n=63)	5.1
Threats to self (suicidal)	(n=27)	2.2
Odd or peculiar	(n=725)	59.0
Immoral	(n=88)	7.2
No behavior reported by accuser or witnesses	(n=10)	0.8
		100.0

constructed so as to *minimize* the number of merely "odd or peculiar," or "immoral" individuals.

Two-thirds of all those committed were odd, peculiar, or simply immoral individuals who displayed no symptoms indicating serious disability, or violent or destructive tendencies. The reported behavior of this 66 percent included primarily nervous and depressive symptoms and a wide variety of fears, beliefs, perceptions, and delusions. In these cases the examiners noted the behavior which they and various witnesses deemed inappropriate, but failed to indicate any reason why the individual, for his own protection or that of the community, had to be detained.

The sociologist Thomas Scheff has termed this odd or peculiar behavior "residual deviance," as opposed to the "explicit deviance" of "immoral behavior." Residually deviant behavior, which Scheff perhaps erroneously considers to be the typical behavior of those labeled "mentally ill" today, is not like that of criminals, prostitutes, alcoholics, or sexual deviants, because it transgresses cultural norms that have no explicit name. Nonetheless those norms are essential to the culture's sense of reality. A residually deviant person is labeled mentally ill, according to Scheff, when his behavior is perceived to be out of touch with the reality that "normal" people take so much for granted that they need not ordinarily define it. One becomes legally insane, further, when a court lends official sanction to that label.

Scheff's category of "residual deviance" is quite useful for grasping the type of disorder characteristic of a certain proportion of the insane—those whose behavior is "odd" or "peculiar"—even though, as numerous defenders of the "medical model" have pointed out, such behavior may nevertheless have hidden physiological origins. Peculiar behavior, as Scheff notes, does constitute a threat to implicit canons of normality. But Scheff's analysis, like much "interactionist" sociology, neglects the historical and structural matrices in which peculiar behavior occurs. He thus fails to examine the concrete modes of behavior that seem peculiar in this particular society—a bourgeois society. Moreover, he overlooks the fact that many residual deviants were labeled "insane" and subsequently committed not simply because their behavior challenged vital, implicit social rules, but because they were a genuine burden for families with limited resources in a society without state-financed welfare.

On the other hand, the San Francisco commitment records do support a modified labeling perspective, one based upon the centrality of the "convenience function" of the commitment system. In the early twentieth century those individuals labeled insane appear typically to have been neither seriously disabled nor dangerous to be at large; rather, they seem to have been bothersome individuals—some mentally ill, some not—whose institutionalization was sought by acquaintances or officials and facilitated by state policy. This perspective has the advantage of permitting us to account for the 7 percent of those labeled insane in San Francisco who were actually, in Scheff's terms, "explicit" deviants.[6]

It might be argued that in those cases in which the accused expressed a willingness to go to the hospital voluntarily, the examiner should not be expected to have demonstrated the "need" for detention; the accused himself presumably acknowledged the need, although it seems likely that he often simply acquiesced in a decision taken by relatives—one that he may not have fully understood. Indeed, it is a mistake to assume that a clear boundary separated involuntary from voluntary commitment. As recent studies have pointed out, those persons alleged to be mentally ill typically undergo intense pressures—not only from medical personnel, but from other officials and family members—to submit voluntarily to therapeutic intervention. The implicit, and

6. Scheff, *Being Mentally Ill*, p. 34. Andrew T. Scull offers a perceptive critique of labeling theory in the first chapter of *Decarceration—A Radical View* (Englewood Cliffs, N.J., 1977). He notes that "labeling theorists continue to apply an interactionist viewpoint"—one that centers on the interaction between discrete individuals apart from sociopolitical context— "where a structural analysis is called for" (p. 11). The extended debate among sociologists over Scheff's formulation of the "labeling theory" may be followed in three recent articles: Scheff, "The Labelling Theory of Mental Illness," *American Sociological Review* 39 (June 1974), 444-452; Walter Gove, "Individual Resources and Mental Hospitalization: A Comparison and Evaluation of the Societal Reaction and Psychiatric Perspectives," *American Sociological Review* 39 (February 1974), 86-100; and Gove, "Who is Hospitalized: A Critical Review of Some Sociological Studies of Mental Illness," *Journal of Health and Social Behavior* 11 (1970), 294-303. See also the two recent collections: Scheff, ed., *Labeling Madness* (Englewood Cliffs, N.J., 1975), and Gove, ed., *The Labelling of Deviance* (New York, 1975).

sometimes explicit, message is: you may accede to treatment willingly; if you do not, you will be committed involuntarily. Coercion is clearly compatible with formally "voluntary" treatment. Dr. Stocking, Superintendent of Agnews State Hospital, provided firm, if unintended, support for that conclusion when he wrote in 1915 that "the majority of cases that are committed *are made to* feel that their presence [in the hospital] is essential to their mental and physical health, and when they *are made to* feel this, they become contented and this feeling makes possible curative work that would otherwise be impossible."[7]

Nevertheless, even if we omit all the "voluntary patients"—of whom 40 percent (25 sample members) were residual ("odd or peculiar") deviants—we may still conclude that 61 percent of the involuntarily committed insane population (56 percent residual deviants and 5 percent explicit deviants) appear not to have been "so far disordered in mind" that they were "dangerous to be at large."

In at least six out of ten cases, therefore, it was the presence of socially inappropriate behavior that constituted the actual grounds for commitment, although such commitment was contrary to a strict reading of the commitment law. It is true that beginning in 1911 county judges in California could legally commit ordinary alcoholics and drug addicts to state hospitals for limited terms of treatment. But these commitments were not for "insanity"; they were for "intemperance." This "progressive" measure drew outraged protests from hospital superintendents once it became clear that the counties were unloading unexpectedly large numbers of these explicit deviants on their institutions. The superintendents argued that mixing such patent undesirables with

7. Miller, *Managing Madness*, pp. 16-18, 86-87; Leonard Stocking, "Agnews State Hospital," 6 *St. Bd. Char. and Corr.* 1915, p. 101. Italics added.

their mental patients undermined their efforts at therapy.[8]

From 1911 to 1920 between 250 and 350 San Franciscans were committed under the intemperance law each year; during Prohibition the number fell to approximately 75 annually. Over the entire period from 1906 to 1930—during which 12,765 San Franciscans were committed for insanity—2,945 individuals were committed for intemperance. But since records of commitments under the Inebriety Law were bound separately, none of those commitments are included in my sample. What is of utmost interest, therefore, is that so many of those committed for *insanity* (at least 3 percent after 1911), and included in my sample, were—to judge by the record—nothing more than alcoholics or drug addicts.[9]

If the individuals committed for insanity by the San Francisco Superior Court posed a threat, it was ordinarily not a threat to other persons, property, or themselves, but to articulated moral norms, to the culture's underlying sense of "reality," or to the peace and tranquility of their relatives, neighbors, or public officials. The primary function of insane commitments was in fact, though not in statute, the socialization of troubling behavior: the provision of state-financed detention and custodial care for persons who allegedly could no longer function independently or "get along" with their families, neighbors, or urban officials.

III

The various types of behavior reported to the examiners —as well as the forms of behavior observed in the Detention Hospital itself—were not evenly distributed

8. See the State Commissioner in Lunacy's report on the "Inebriates," 8 *St. Comm. Lun.* 1912, pp. 12-17.

9. The gross figures on intemperance commitments under the Inebriety Law were tabulated from the San Francisco Board of Supervisors, "County Clerk Report," *San Francisco Municipal Reports* (San Francisco, annual).

among all insane individuals. Important variations—by sex, nativity, family, and class—were evident. Particularly in the case of the examiners' observations, the frequency of morally judgmental rhetoric varied directly with some key determinants of the individual's social position.

The medical examiners recorded in three-quarters of the cases a brief observation of the accused person's behavior while in detention: 3 percent of the observations referred to actions (e.g., "bothers other patients," "won't answer questions"), 7 percent referred to a symptom or diagnosis ("mutism," "apoplexy"), and a small number to a belief (e.g., "believes doctors harming her"). But in nine out of ten cases the examiners recorded a simple—often morally judgmental—observation concerning a habit, temperamental trait, or innate quality of the accused.

Table 12 gives the characteristics most commonly observed by the San Francisco medical examiners. When we consider precisely who was described as "good," "intelligent," or "inferior," we discover that the male, the unskilled, the foreign-born, the most recent immigrants, and those with no relatives in the city were significantly more likely to be judged in a disapproving way.

Women, for example, made up 56 percent of the "good," and 68 percent of the "intelligent," but only 19 percent of the "inferior." Some of this variation can perhaps be explained by their overrepresentation among those with relatives, who as a group were distinctly more liable to obtain recorded observations of both "intelligent" and "good." Thus 95 percent of the "intelligent" and 80 percent of the "good" had kin in the city. Conversely, two-thirds of the "inferior" had no relatives in San Francisco. Perhaps the examiners tried especially in the presence of relatives to make a kindly comment about the accused.

Table 12

BEHAVIORAL CHARACTERISTICS MOST COMMONLY OBSERVED
BY MEDICAL EXAMINERS, 1906-1929

Characteristics	Times reported	As percent of all observed behavior
Quiet, retiring	(409)	30.9
Good	(213)	16.1
Nervous, excitable	(97)	7.3
Average	(95)	7.2
Intelligent	(60)	4.5
Inferior mentality	(48)	3.6
Jolly, joyful	(47)	3.6
Quick-tempered	(42)	3.2
Won't answer	(30)	2.3
Neurotic temperament	(25)	1.9
Dull	(18)	1.4
		82.0

On the other hand, the designation "inferior" may have been applied more frequently to men because they were very overrepresented among those whose reported behavior fit into the category of explicit deviance. Men made up 70 percent of all alcoholics and 90 percent of all those reported masturbating or syphilitic, though they accounted for only 60 percent of those for whom some behavior was reported. Seven in ten explicit deviants—that is, all those with reportedly immoral habits—were men.[10]

10. It is interesting to note that while reports of alcoholism diminished slightly during Prohibition, and reports of syphilis rose somewhat after 1914—probably because of the widespread adoption of the Wasserman diagnostic test, first mentioned in the records in 1912—use of the masturbation category declined substantially after World War I. It made up 12

A second major correlate of "inferior" or "intelligent" ratings was occupational position. The unskilled laborers, who received only 14 percent of the total observations, accounted for 47 percent of the inferior ratings and 32 percent of the "dull." Of the intelligent ratings, by contrast, one-third were low white-collar—an occupational group that received only 16 percent of the total observations.

The unskilled laborers, interestingly, did not make up a disproportionate share of the explicit deviants; we cannot claim that the morally judgmental observations of the examiners in this case derived from reported immoral behavior. Although the unskilled were more likely to be reported masturbating than other occupational groups, they were not distinctly liable to be alcoholic or syphilitic—in fact, the white-collar accused were much more frequently syphilitic than any blue-collar group.

The medical examiners' tendency to label the unskilled "inferior" would appear to be a consequence, rather, of the nativity of this occupational group. While seven in ten of the intelligent were native-born, seven in ten of the inferior were foreign-born—though foreigners ac-

percent of the total between 1906 and 1916, 8 percent between 1918 and 1928, but only 3.8 percent between 1924 and 1928. It would appear that by the end of the twenties autoeroticism was no longer considered quite so frequently to be an indication of mental or nervous disorder. Similarly, statewide statistics on the causes of insanity among admitted patients between 1861 and 1920 show a steady decline in the proportion of cases said to be caused by masturbation. From 10 percent in 1861 the proportion declines to 8 percent in 1883, 7 percent in 1891, 6 percent in 1902, 4 percent in 1908, 2 percent in 1914, and 0.5 percent in 1920. (Figures tabulated from reports of individual hospitals and, after 1898, of the State Commission in Lunacy.) On "masturbatory insanity," see Dr. John W. Robertson, "Relation Existing Between the Sexual Organs and Insanity, with Especial Reference to Masturbation," *Transactions of the Medical Society of the State of California* 28 (1898), 254-261, and R. P. Neuman, "Masturbation, Madness, and the Modern Concepts of Childhood and Adolescence," *Journal of Social History* 8 (Spring 1975), 1-27.

counted for only 45 percent of those about whom observations were recorded. Of the eighteen "intelligent" foreigners in the sample, furthermore, only one was Irish and only two were Italians—which suggests that the examiners considered Catholic foreigners the least intelligent of all. Significantly, two-thirds of the "dull" were native-born, which raises the possibility that those natives with limited mental capacity—and who were more likely to have relatives on the scene—were commonly accorded a label considerably less demeaning than "inferior."

Catholics as a group were not as underrepresented as foreigners among the intelligent, but they were equally "inferior." A substantial 40 percent of the intelligent were Catholic, but Catholics also comprised 70 percent of the inferior. Jews, ironically, appear to have been over-represented among both the intelligent and the inferior. They accounted for 13 percent of the intelligent, 11 percent of the inferior, but only 7 percent of all those with observations. The nativity of the Jewish insane explains the anomaly. The inferior were almost without exception Russian immigrants, while the intelligent were either native-born or German-born Jews who had been in California for a considerably longer period of time.

We can gain a somewhat more complete picture of the judgmental character of the examiners' observations by grouping them, whenever possible, into either a disapproving or an approving category. Approving terms were "good," "intelligent," "temperate," "jolly," or "joyful." Disapproving terms included "inferior," "disobedient," "violent," "peculiar," "wild," "dissolute," "dull," "abusive," "silly," "stubborn," and "lazy." Of all of the observed characteristics that could be grouped in either category, 17 percent were disapproving and 83 percent were approving. But of the observations given to those without relatives, 28 percent were disapproving; individuals with relatives received disapproving observations only 10 percent of the time. Observations about the unskilled were 30 percent disapproving, compared to 13 percent for the white-collar accused. Of the foreign-born as a whole, 21 percent were disapproving, compared to 13 percent for the natives. Yet of the recently arrived or non-white immigrants, the proportion was higher: 40 percent disapproving for the Asians and Mexicans, 25 percent for the Russians, and 24 percent for the Italians. Only 6 percent of the observations made about women were disapproving; men received negative judgments nearly 20 percent of the time.

We lack an adequate number of cases to be able to distinguish more precisely the respective influences of relatives, nativity, occupation, and sex, but we can state with confidence that the medical examiners' observations—rendered in a hurried, perfunctory manner—tended to be more negative, even demeaning, when the accused was either male, foreign-born, unskilled, recently arrived, non-white, or without family in San Francisco.[11]

IV

On the basis of the reported and observed behavior displayed by the accused, the examiners were supposed to offer a diagnosis and a judgment concerning the cause of insanity. In fact, they rarely offered a diagnosis and they speculated about causation in only one-quarter of the cases. No more than 6 percent of the accused were diagnosed—usually with standard clinical designations such as "dementia praecox," "senile dementia," or "gen-

11. Recent research supports the finding that psychiatric observers render judgments not only on clinical, but also on social and cultural, grounds. See M. Bloombaum *et al.*, "Cultural Stereotyping Among Psychotherapists," *Journal of Consulting Clinical Psychologists* 32 (1968), 99-117; S. M. Miller and E. G. Mishler, "Social Class, Mental Illness, and American Psychiatry," *Milbank Memorial Fund Quarterly* 37 (1959), 174-199; and David Mechanic, *Mental Health and Social Policy* (Englewood Cliffs, N.J., 1969), p. 106.

eral paralysis of the insane." The examiners appear clearly to have been incapable of judging the precise "form" of insanity—both because they did not take the necessary time to establish a preliminary diagnosis and because, as general practitioners, they may have felt unprepared to try.

Whatever the reason, the state hospital superintendents bewailed the practice of committing people without any effort to diagnose the disorder. "The examiners [in San Francisco]," complained Dr. Elmer Stone of the Napa State Hospital, "do not pretend to make a diagnosis—they leave that matter entirely to us at the hospital. There are often patients committed to our institution from . . . San Francisco . . . who should never have been sent to the institution, and that is due largely to the fault of the examiners in being hasty."[12]

In assigning causes of insanity the examiners actually became less venturesome during the course of the quarter century covered by the records. Three-quarters of the total assigned causes were given to the one-half of the accused who were committed between 1906 and 1918; 58 percent of all causes were recorded between 1906 and 1914, but only 35 percent of the sample was committed during that period. Clearly the examiners were more confident of their capacity to render etiological judgments before the war than after. It must have seemed increasingly plain to the general practitioner that only a professional psychiatrist could pronounce upon such matters. The American Psychiatric Association—founded in 1921—doubtless did its best to foster that conviction.

An examination of which accused individuals received the various "causes" is quite revealing, even though three-quarters of the sample members were assigned no cause at all. As in the case of the recorded behavior, the

12. Dr. Elmer Stone, "Comments," 4 *Cal. St. Conf. Char. and Corr. 1906,* p. 152.

distribution of causes varies according to the presence of relatives, nativity, occupation, religion, and, most notably, sex.

Seven of every ten assigned causes fit into the general category of what were commonly called "physical" causes. One-quarter came under the rubric of "moral" causes, and the remainder were termed "heredity"—a "cause" that contained both physical and moral elements.[13] In the first group syphilis (16 percent of the total), alcoholism (13 percent), old age (7 percent), drug habit (5 percent), and menopause (5 percent) figured most prominently. Among moral causes, mental or nervous shock (12 percent of the total) and financial difficulties (5 percent) were the most common.

Those individuals accused by relatives, or who had relatives in the city, were much more likely to have a moral cause. On the other hand, those accused by doctors or police, or without relatives in San Francisco, received a very disproportionate share of the physical causes. This clear-cut contrast is no doubt in part the result of the high concentration of alcoholics and syphilitics among those without relatives who were accused by police and doctors. But it may also be partly explained by the fact that relatives would in all likelihood have sought to comprehend or portray the affliction as a case of unexpected shock—as an environmental intrusion—rather than as a personal or familial failing. In fact, 30 percent of the 76 cases of "mental shock" among sample members were traced directly to the earthquake of 1906; that event was still being cited as a "cause" of insanity even after World War I.

13. The State Commission in Lunacy employed the designations "physical," "moral," and "heredity" in its biennial statistical summary of state hospital admissions. Although heredity accounted for less than 10 percent of the causes cited by the examiners, we should not conclude that they considered heredity to play no part in the genesis of the other cases. In fact, heredity was assumed to be at least a "predisposing" cause in the vast majority of cases.

The assignment of moral and physical causes was linked not only to the presence of relatives, but also—and probably more directly—to sex. Men and women were proportionately represented among those receiving causes (56 percent were male, 44 percent female), but seven in ten physical causes went to men and seven in ten moral causes went to women. Put another way, while 70 percent of all causes were physical, almost 90 percent of those attributed to men were physical, compared to 50 percent of those attributed to women. The only physical cause which was more common among women than men was old age; women made up 60 percent of all such cases. This disproportion, as I argued in Chapter Five, can be partly explained by the fact that state hospitals for the insane were the only public "shelters" capable of caring permanently for aged, dependent women. With the exception of old age, no other physical cause came close to being as common among females as among males.

Women also predominated, as we would expect, among those whose insanity was "hereditary," comprising more than half of those assigned this cause. Other groups with a disproportionate tendency toward hereditary insanity were the native-born, the white-collar, and the Jewish. More than seven in ten were native-born, compared to less than six in ten of all those with an assigned cause. More than half were white-collar, compared to less than one-quarter of all those with a recorded cause. More than 16 percent were Jewish, against only 6 percent of those given causes. We would expect natives to predominate in this fashion, since the examiners could discover more about their relatives and their heredity. But it is not so clear why the white-collar and the Jewish should stand out. Perhaps white-collar individuals were more willing to discuss previous mental disturbances within the family, or quicker to recognize that they existed. Contemporary studies of mental disorder do in fact suggest that those from higher occupational strata are more likely to trace mental problems to family environment than those from lower strata.[14]

In the case of the Jews, it was a well-worn truism in the medical literature of the early twentieth century that they had suffered for generations from "delusions of persecution." It would not be surprising if the examiners —or even some Jews themselves—tended to attribute their present disorders to "heredity"—a term that then tended to denote not just "genetic" but also cultural and familial inheritance.[15]

On the other hand, not a single Jew displayed a disorder caused by alcohol, drugs, or old age. Drug abuse, interestingly, was very disproportionately a "Protestant" cause, whereas alcoholism was usually a "Catholic" cause: 60 percent of those with a drug habit as the recorded cause of insanity were Protestant, compared to 45 percent of all those with an assigned cause. Two-thirds of those whose insanity was caused by alcoholism were Catholic, and more than 20 percent were born in Ireland.

14. J. K. Myers and B. H. Roberts, *Family and Class Dynamics in Mental Illness* (New York, 1959), p. 204 and *passim*; W. S. Williams, "Class Differences in the Attitudes of Psychiatric Patients," *Social Problems* 4 (January 1957), 240-244; I. Zola, "Illness Behavior of the Working Class," in A. Shostak and W. Gomberg, eds., *Blue-Collar World* (Englewood Cliffs, N.J., 1964), pp. 351-361; Sally Guttmacher and Jack Elinson, "Ethno-Religious Variation in Perceptions of Illness," *Social Science and Medicine* 5 (1971), 117-125; Marvin Opler and Jerome Singer, "Ethnic Differences in Behavior and Psychopathology: Italian and Irish," *International Journal of Social Psychiatry* 2 (Summer 1956), 11-22.

15. "By reason of his history the Jew is usually more neurotic than his neighbor." "Insanity Among the Jews," *Philadelphia Medical Journal* 6 (December 8, 1900), 1074-1075. See also A. Myerson, "The 'Nervousness' of the Jew," *Mental Hygiene* 4 (January 1920), 65-72; Frank G. Hyde, "Notes on the Hebrew Insane," *American Journal of Insanity* 58 (January 1902), 469-471; and Benjamin Malzberg, "The Prevalence of Mental Disease Among Jews," *Mental Hygiene* 14 (October 1930), 926-946.

It is important to stress, however, that in three-quarters of the cases the medical examiners felt incapable of positing a cause of insanity (or neglected to do so), and that in more than 90 percent of the cases they were unable to offer a preliminary diagnosis. To be sure, the practice of screening patients at the Detention Hospital as quickly as possible virtually ruled out such judgments. Yet even the few detainees sent for up to two weeks to the Psychopathic Ward after 1923 frequently returned to the Detention Hospital without a diagnosis. As the state hospital superintendents acknowledged, it often took months even for doctors with years of experience to arrive at a diagnosis.[16]

Even if the examiners had had more time, it seems unlikely that their observations would have been more precise. For, as the records of reported and observed behavior suggest, a full two-thirds of all those persons labeled insane exhibited neither a severely disabling disturbance nor violent or destructive tendencies. They were more than 60 percent of the time residual or explicit deviants whose behavior, in the eyes of witnesses and examiners, was either immoral, out of touch with the reality that "normal" people took for granted, or simply too burdensome for relatives, acquaintances, or public officials to bear.

16. Dr. F. W. Hatch, "Comments," 4 *Cal. St. Conf. Char. and Corr.* 1906, p. 159.

7

"Normal" Mental Illness and the "Defective" Insane

The commitment of more than 12,000 individuals in San Francisco between 1906 and 1929 was not, it must be stressed, the result of a campaign by the medical profession or any other elite group to deprive innocent victims of their liberty or to "restore social control." The temptation is strong to reduce the history of social welfare and of the "helping professions" to a morality play pitting the malignant "controllers" against the poor deviants who sought only to march to the beat of their own drummer. The best way to resist that temptation is to acknowledge that, despite the medical profession's easily documented effort to increase its control over the commitment process, local authorities and the families of the insane themselves continued to use the process for their own ends. For the insane were a threat not to social order in the abstract, but in many cases to the "public order" of their neighborhoods and the tranquility and financial survival of their families. The "helping professions" and the institutions for incarcerating deviants did take over from the family and the local community the responsibility of caring for troublesome charges, but they did not—as is often implied in the literature of "social control"—simply muscle the family or community aside. Those traditional units frequently cooperated in the transformation, and reaped some immediate benefits from it.

This chapter will attempt to deal, in an admittedly rudimentary way, with a related and very complex issue: the relationship between the commitment process and cultural attitudes toward insanity—attitudes characteristic not simply of medical specialists, but of a wider reading public and of a still broader population containing most of those who petitioned for the commitment of their relatives, friends, and acquaintances.

The quarter-century covered by the San Francisco commitment records was a period of striking change, it would seem, in both popular and medical assumptions about the nature of mental disorder and the proper means of responding to it. While it is difficult to be precise in measuring popular attitudes toward mental illness, it would seem apparent that after 1910 and especially by the 1920s, a sizable segment of the public believed that mental or nervous disorder could affect even "normal" persons, and that seeking professional help in an urban treatment facility carried little or none of the stigma traditionally associated with insane asylums. In 1929, after two decades of mass publicity concerning "mental hygiene," the number of individual "visits" recorded in the "psychiatric departments of general hospitals" in San Francisco, according to a study by the American Public Health Association, was 20,572, including 1,669 new cases (669 of them children) in the fiscal year 1929-1930.[1]

But what was the connection between the emerging attitude of tolerance toward mental disorder, the consequent readiness of many disturbed individuals to seek or accept treatment locally, and the commitment process? Were people with mental problems less liable by the 1920s to encounter the demand that they be confined

---

1. Ira V. Hiscock, *An Appraisal of the Public Health Program, San Francisco, California, for the Fiscal Year 1929-1930* (San Francisco, 1930), p. 104. This figure probably does not represent 20,572 individuals, since one patient could probably "visit" a facility more than once each year.

indefinitely in a state hospital? There is no doubt that the number of San Franciscans committed in the 1920s did not keep pace with the increase in population. In that decade the adult population of the city rose 25 percent, yet the annual number of commitments was relatively constant, and even somewhat lower than during the peak years between 1914 and 1919. The annual average for the 1920s was 570, compared to 608 annually for the war years.[2]

This reduction did not stem from any greater willingness on the part of the medical examiners to release allegedly insane persons from the Detention Hospital. The ratio of those committed to those examined remained in the 1920s at the same high level of 80 percent that it had reached in 1914. The key to the decline in the commitment figures in the 1920s is that while the number of adults in the city rose by one-quarter, the number of affidavits of insanity filed in the Superior Court did not rise at all. In 1915, 734 San Franciscans were officially charged with insanity; in 1929 an identical 734 were charged, the first time in the postwar years that the 1915 figure had been reached. During the 1920s accusations averaged 687 per year.[3]

The drop in accusations and the resulting failure of commitments to keep pace with population is probably explained by the availability of voluntary outpatient and to a modest extent in-patient care in the city itself. By 1922 San Francisco had four outpatient psychiatric clinics for the general public; the largest—the state-financed University of California Psychiatric Clinic—saw 800 patients in its first two years of operation (fiscal 1920-1922). Two outpatient psychological clinics, including the Mental Hygiene Clinic of the California Society for Mental Hygiene—which saw 445 patients in its first 10

2. For the San Francisco commitment figures, see Table 2, p. 36.
3. The affidavit figures are contained in the County Clerk's Report, *San Francisco Municipal Reports* (San Francisco, annual).

months of service beginning in 1917—were also in operation. By the mid-1920s some in-patients could receive voluntary care without leaving the city. Precise figures on the number of "voluntary" patients admitted to the San Francisco County Hospital Psychopathic Ward—patients, that is, not referred to the ward by the Detention Hospital—could not be found. Dr. Edward Twitchell, Director of the Psychopathic Ward, reported to the Department of Public Health in February 1925 that 164 patients had been admitted in the previous five months, "of whom many are voluntary." But the number of voluntary patients was probably no more than about 100 per year, since a total of only 108 of the 345 treated at the ward in the fiscal year 1924-1925 were said to have been "discharged to their homes after a brief period of medical care and rest in this ward." Stanford Medical School's Hospital, the only private hospital in the city accepting mental patients for extended care in the 1920s, admitted 627 patients to its 23-bed mental ward in 1929.[4]

Despite the proportional reduction in the *number* of persons committed to state hospitals in the 1920s, however, the *types* of persons committed remained unchanged: the insane population still comprised the same broad array of odd, peculiar, or immoral deviants, in addition to some seriously disabled individuals. Commitments in the 1920s were no more restricted to "well-defined" mental diseases than they had been before or during the war. The apparent increase in tolerance for the mentally ill did not lead to a restriction of state hospital commitments to the "dangerously" disordered

4. 1 *Cal. Dept. Instits.* 1923, p. 31; Elsie Krafft, *The Mental Hygiene Clinic* (San Francisco, 1918), p. 3; Department of Public Health, *Minute Books*, February 19, 1925, p. 3677; *Annual Report of the Department of Public Health, 1924-1925* (San Francisco, 1925), p. 51; Federick H. Allen, *Mental Hygiene Survey of the State of California* (Sacramento, 1932), p. 141.

or severely incapacitated. Counties in California continued to unload hundreds of "undesirables" each year on
state mental institutions. Toleration was selective: it
seems to have been extended to those "mentally ill"
persons who showed signs, through their willingness to
seek therapy voluntarily, of aspiring to remain or become "productive" members of the community.

II

By the 1920s the term "mentally ill" seems in fact to
have been increasingly used to connote those who were
not committed, who merited sympathy precisely because
they struggled to maintain their "social efficiency" even
while temporarily afflicted. The "mentally ill" were to be
dissociated from the "insane," who were "defectives" in
need of confinement and in many cases sterilization.
Though "insanity" was of course still considered an
extreme form of "mental illness," the latter label now
began to imply a wide range of "mild" disorders that
were compatible with a respectable place in society.

In 1914, for example, the *Literary Digest* noted the
"passing of 'insanity'" as the term had been previously
understood. Quoting approvingly from the nationally
prominent psychiatrist William A. White, Superintendent of the Government Hospital for the Insane in
Washington, D.C., the *Digest* expressed the view that
"not all the mentally diseased are insane." While "insanity" would continue to designate "a certain type of social
lack of adaptation and a certain kind of conduct which
renders the individual incapable of getting along in the
community," it was not to be equated with mental
illness. For "there are many persons suffering from
mental disease who get along efficiently in the community, and who are not insane and could not be so
designated." Mental illness no longer had to imply
incapacity or profound alienation from the community
of normally functioning individuals. In many cases it

could signify a temporary, treatable upset in a person whose "efficient" functioning would be interrupted only briefly, if at all. On the other hand, "the word 'insanity,'" as Dr. White declared in a 1915 address, "is not a medical term at all, but a social term which defines a certain kind of socially inefficient conduct."[5]

The emergence of the new attitude of toleration for "mental illness" was clearly related—perhaps both as cause and as effect—to the growth of the medical view that "acute" disorders, in the treatment of which psychopathic wards were to specialize, were commonplace and curable. These relatively minor disturbances still required professional treatment, medical men urged, but they did not imply insanity. "'Nervous and mental illness' distinctly does *not* connote 'insanity,'" announced an article in the official organ of the American Psychiatric Association in 1926. "Today no well-informed person believes the problem of mental health to be one merely of 'insanity.' The realization is steadily growing that insanity, so-called, is but a later stage in a psychopathologic process, and that the larger number of those who are mentally ill and in need of expert medical attention are not 'insane.'"[6]

Of course it was in the self-interest of the psychiatric professionals to foster the view that many sane individuals were nevertheless in need of psychiatric treatment. But articles in popular magazines and newspapers— along with a growing public use of psychiatric clinics— suggest the conclusion that far from artificially stimulating a demand for its services, professional psychiatry was at least in part responding to a widespread plea for active measures to protect the mental health of the population.

5. "Passing of 'Insanity,'" *Literary Digest* 48 (March 21, 1914), 616; William A. White, "The Meaning of the Mental Hygiene Movement," *Boston Medical and Surgical Journal* 175 (August 14, 1916), 264-265.

6. George K. Pratt, "Psychiatric Departments in General Hospitals," *American Journal of Psychiatry* 5 (January, 1926) 403-404. Italics in original.

Psychiatrists did clearly attempt to channel public sentiment by discounting or discrediting alternative modes of
"treatment," such as the Emmanuel Movement, New
Thought, and Christian Science—precisely by insisting
that mental disturbances were primarily medical, not
spiritual, problems. Yet the proliferation of therapies—
even of those opposed by psychiatrists—is in itself
evidence of the growing popular demand for the treatment of what were increasingly perceived as a group of
common and relatively minor disorders.[7]

The First World War appears to have been a critical
period in the growing acceptance of the broader view of
mental illness. An immense wartime literature revealed
that a large number of soldiers—whether in combat or
not—suffered from various neuroses subsumed under
the label "shell shock." "As knowledge about shell shock
spread," notes John C. Burnham, "the public became
increasingly aware that one's mind could play tricks . . .
and produce neurotic symptoms. . . . By turning the
neurosis into a war wound, the experience of World War
I mitigated public attitudes toward mental illnesses more
effectively than years of humanitarian propaganda."[8]

For over a decade the organized mental hygiene
movement had been agitating for a more sympathetic
approach to the mentally disturbed, for a recognition

7. An indispensable account of the popular demand for therapy—
psychiatric and non-psychiatric—is that of Nathan G. Hale, Jr., who ex-
amines "mind cures and the mystical wave: popular preparation for psychoanalysis, 1904-1910," in his *Freud and the Americans* (New York, 1971),
pp. 225-249. See also Donald Meyer's original study of mind cure in *The
Positive Thinkers* (Garden City, N.Y., 1965), Part One. For a typical psychiatric put-down of Christian Science, see the editorial "Insanity and Christian
Science," *American Journal of Insanity* 57 (April, 1901), 726-727.

8. John Chynoweth Burnham, "The New Psychology: From Narcissism
to Social Control," in John Braeman *et al.*, eds., *Change and Continuity in
Twentieth Century America: The 1920's* (Columbus, Ohio, 1968), p. 362. A
typical wartime analysis is Frederick W. Parsons, "War Neuroses," *Atlantic
Monthly* 123 (March, 1919), 335-338.

that transitory disorders could afflict even Yale-educated businessmen like Clifford Beers—who founded the National Committee for Mental Hygiene in 1909 after his release from a mental hospital. The war experience revealed that not only "normal" but also "heroic" individuals might be unexpectedly afflicted for a time. "Thousands of men," the *Examiner* editorialized in 1919, "have come out of their service in the army with shattered nervous systems which have directly affected them mentally. . . . These are not necessarily insane, but rather unstable mentally and nervously." Their disability was "easily traceable to its initiating causes," and could, "without difficulty in many cases, be eradicated." Support for an expansion of psychiatric services mushroomed during and after the war. In San Francisco four psychiatric clinics and four psychological clinics were established between 1917 and 1920.[9]

By the 1920s the widespread prevalence of "neurosis" —which on the whole no longer signified organic nerve disease but rather any minor mental or nervous disturbance—was taken for granted. Certainly the popularization of Freud's notions on the "psychopathology of everyday life" played a part in this development. But Freud became popular, as Nathan Hale has shown, because the educated public had been prepared for his work over a period of decades—dating back at least to the publication of George M. Beard's *American Nervousness* in 1881. As Adolf Meyer, the dean of American psychiatrists, suggested, the rise of urban neurological practice in the late nineteenth century clearly adumbrated the mental hygiene movement in its broad effort to treat a wide range of disorders exhibited by "those not glaringly 'insane.'" Any form of disturbance "that could be somehow worked with under the appearance of

9. "California Should Establish a Psychopathic Hospital," Editorial, *San Francisco Examiner*, March 22, 1919, p. 18. See also, "Rehabilitation of Disabled Soldiers," *San Francisco Chronicle*, August 11, 1918, p. 18.

cooperation with the patient tended to be drawn under the heading of nerves [or] neurasthenia." Readers of national magazines were aware well before the Freudian vogue that Americans were suffering from "nervous and mental ills which . . . may not culminate in insanity."[10] The contribution of Freud was not in pointing out the existence of widespread neurotic tendencies, but in suggesting a novel interpretation of their origins and a new method of treatment. At the same time, the vigorous debate over Freud's ideas—especially those on human sexuality—put the subject of neurosis all the more at the center of public attention.[11]

The medical focus on acute disorders, the crusade for preventive mental hygiene, the wartime experience, and the debate over Freud all contributed to the new popular attitude of the 1920s. Clear signs of the shift were apparent in California during the war. In 1918 Superintendent Robert Richards of the Mendocino State Hospital commented that "general experience and observation anywhere in any community will show the toleration and usefulness of [many of those with] unrecognized, undiagnosed mental abnormalities."[12] Such testi-

10. Adolf Meyer, "Organization of Community Facilities for Prevention, Care, and Treatment of Nervous and Mental Diseases," in Frankwood E. Williams, ed., *Proceedings of the First International Congress on Mental Hygiene, Washington, D.C., 1930*, vol. 1 (New York, 1932), p. 239; H. Addington Bruce, "Insanity and the Nation," *North American Review* 187 (January 1908), 73.

11. Hale, *Freud and the Americans*, pp. 47-68; Charles E. Rosenberg, "The Place of George M. Beard in Nineteenth Century Psychiatry," *Bulletin of the History of Medicine* 36 (1962), 245-259.

12. Robert L. Richards, "Report of the Medical Superintendent," 11 *St. Comm. Lun.* 1918, p. 56. It is interesting to note that the term "neurosis" —first used in the nineteenth century to indicate an organic disease of the nervous system—was first indexed in the *Reader's Guide to Periodical Literature* in the late 1920s, when it was securely rooted in popular usage as a label for relatively minor mental or nervous disorders. George Gerbner, "Psychology, Psychiatry and Mental Illness in the Mass Media: A Study of Trends, 1900-1959," *Mental Hygiene* 45 (January 1961), 91.

mony to the continued productive capacities of persons suffering from mental disturbances had never before occurred in the reports of the State Commission in Lunacy or the State Board of Charities and Corrections. As early as 1915, Dr. Ray Lyman Wilbur could casually state to the Commonwealth Club of San Francisco that he knew of "active men in the community" and "mothers with children and large families" who had suffered, and recovered, from mental disorders. In 1917 the *San Francisco Examiner*, in a feature article on the current "wave of psychotherapy" in the city, argued that not only some, but most, westerners had become "neurotic"—a usage that, however exaggerated, implies that the paper's readers understood the concept and considered it a common phenomenon.[13]

By the end of the 1920s, a psychologist attempting to define insanity in *Current History* could announce that America had entered "the psychopathic era," in which "the dividing area between the normal and the abnormal loses its sharp boundaries. . . . The variations within the normal range find their interpretation in the more pronounced issues of the abnormal." He could claim that "the recognition of the wide prevalence of minor mental disqualifications—the phobias and hesitations, the obsessions and compulsions, the inferiorities and maladjustments, the complexes and fixations" was responsible for this "momentous advance." "Within a generation we find ourselves thinking of sanity and insanity in wholly novel ways." As Adolf Meyer put it in 1930, a "dynamic" conception had for two decades pervaded American psychiatry, a conception that located "the psychopathological both outside and within so-called

13. Dr. Ray Lyman Wilbur, "Remarks on 'The County Hospital Problem,'" *Transactions of the Commonwealth Club of California* 10 (July 1915), 332-333; Bailey Miller, "How Psychology Will Normalize the Race," *San Francisco Examiner*, February 19, 1917, p. 16.

insanity."[14] The realization that minor mental or nervous disturbances were widespread, might affect anyone, and need not in all or even most cases undermine productive living, represented a major shift in the cultural understanding of insanity. The blurring of the boundary line between normal and abnormal behavior was a development which a host of commentators believed would promote the sympathetic treatment and toleration of disturbed individuals.

But if the blurring of the boundary was capable of stimulating tolerance for those with some form of abnormality, it put an implicit condition upon that tolerance: willingness to enter a therapeutic relationship with a medical authority in the interest of maintaining one's efficiency. Ivan Illich, Christopher Lasch, and others have recently argued that deviant behavior has come in the twentieth century to be tolerated to the extent that deviants acknowledge they are sick and in need of medical management. Confinement in the last half of the century has become increasingly superfluous, as deviants have increasingly accepted the appropriate sick role and perform as cooperative patients. The policy of "deinstitutionalizing" deviants—made necessary by the excessive cost of institutions to financially strapped states, and made possible by the invention and mass production of behavior-controlling drugs—is on the verge of becoming the new national orthodoxy.[15]

14. Joseph Jastrow, "What is Insanity?", *Current History* 29 (December 1928), 406-407; Meyer, "Organization of Community Facilities," p. 241. See Karl Menninger, *The Vital Balance* (New York, 1963), p. 33: "It is now accepted that most people have some degree of mental illness at some time, and may have a degree of mental illness most of the time."

15. Ivan Illich, *Medical Nemesis* (New York, 1976); Andrew T. Scull, *Decarceration—A Radical View* (Englewood Cliffs, N.J., 1977); Nicholas N. Kittrie, *The Right to be Different: Deviance and Enforced Therapy* (Baltimore, 1971); Christopher Lasch, *Haven in a Heartless World* (New York, 1977), esp. pp. 221-222, n. 28; Lasch, "Psychiatry: Call It Teaching or Call It Treatment," *Hastings Center Report* 5 (August 1975), 15-17. Alan A. Stone

In the early twentieth century the first signs of this therapeutic system emerged: individuals exhibiting only minor mental or nervous disorders began in large numbers to desire or accept professional treatment for their conditions. It must be reiterated, however, that expressed willingness to enter a therapeutic relationship is by no means incompatible with a subtle form of coercion—from one's family, associates, and doctors. Granting to a medical or psychiatric authority the responsibility for managing one's behavior and restoring health—surrendering, in other words, one's autonomy—was a condition for remaining in the community. Failure to cooperate would itself signify, in Dr. White's phrase, "a certain kind of socially inefficient conduct"—the mark of the "defective" insane.

III

The explicit distinction that emerged in the early twentieth century between "mental disease" and "insanity"— between a condition in which continued productive functioning was possible and one in which it was clearly impossible—is of utmost interest. For it suggests a further dimension to the argument of the last chapter. What was ultimately distinctive about many individuals committed for insanity was not that they were severely disordered in mind or that they displayed destructive tendencies—the two legal requirements for detention— but that relatives, acquaintances, or public officials considered them *both* bothersome and unproductive, a threat not just to familial or public tranquility, but also to canons of conduct characteristic of bourgeois society. Sanity was equated with rationality and rationality was

----

argues that the recent release of patients from California state hospitals has not in all cases been linked to mandatory outpatient treatment, although that was the announced intention of the deinstitutionalization campaign. *Mental Health and Law*, p. 64.

identified, at bottom, with capacity for and devotion to efficient labor.

Michel Foucault, as noted in the Introduction, has argued that this merging of "madness" and "non-productivity" in Western culture had taken place by the late seventeenth century. The insane, whose madness had previously constituted "a dramatic debate in which [they] confronted the secret powers of the world," were now for the first time systematically confined. This secularization of madness—this denial of the madman's curious, fascinating participation in the mysterious world of spirit—was indispensable, Foucault implies, to the emergence of a bourgeois society in which relationships between individuals, and between land, labor, and capital, were increasingly rationalized. The insane, while lacking in productive capacity or purpose, nevertheless served a potent symbolic function: sequestered in large institutions, they dramatically represented the nonperformance of prescribed social roles, the failure to observe cardinal cultural norms.[16] As Emile Durkheim and some recent sociologists have pointed out, socially deviant behavior should not necessarily be taken as a sign that a society is malfunctioning or "disintegrating"; for such behavior is "a factor in public health, an integral part of all healthy societies." It contributes to the clear, dramatic definition and effective maintenance of basic social norms.[17]

16. Michel Foucault, *Madness and Civilization* (New York, 1965), pp. xi, 61. Other recent writings on the same theme include George Rosen, *Madness in Society* (New York, 1969), especially pp. 151-171; Christopher Lasch, "Origins of the Asylum," *The World of Nations* (New York, 1974), pp. 3-17; E. J. Hundert, "History, Psychology, and the Study of Deviant Behavior," *Journal of Interdisciplinary History* 2 (Spring 1972), especially pp. 470-472.

17. Emile Durkheim, *The Rules of Sociological Method* (Glencoe, Ill., 1938), p. 67; Kai T. Erikson, "Notes on the Sociology of Deviance," *Social Problems* 9 (Spring 1962), 307-314. In Erikson's words, "Deviance cannot be dismissed as behavior which *disrupts* stability in society.... In controlled

It is not possible to demonstrate that the public, or urban officials, or most medical professionals consciously believed that the commitment system was designed to sequester the nonproductive—although doctors did in some cases express that precise opinion. Yet both the San Francisco commitment records and California state publications suggest that this was often an actual, even if not a consciously articulated, function of commitment. The insane person, like the feeble-minded "moron," often possessed "a certain amount of shrewdness and skill"—clearly rational faculties—but he was typically unable to survive in the marketplace, to compete "on equal terms," to manage "his affairs with ordinary prudence." If imprudence was a sign of mental disturbance, idleness was one of its causes. "Idleness induces introspection, the brooding over troubles, the nursing of delusions."[18]

Treatment in the hospital for the insane thus had to take the form of "occupational therapy." Since many patients "have lost perhaps the mental powers necessary to follow their previous occupation . . . it is necessary to re-educate them in some occupation within the reach of their mental capacity." The work should have "some useful end" if possible, but even "work resulting in a poor or useless product is better than idleness." Before and during the First World War the hospital superintendents turned to military drill as a means of further instilling discipline. One superintendent used it "to arouse interest, fix attention, produce orderly action, and willingness to follow direction of others. We have carried it to the extent of a sham battle, and a camping expedition to the mountains,

quantities [it is] an important condition for *preserving* stability." (Page 311, italics in original.) For a contrary view, see M. Harvey Brenner, *Mental Illness and the Economy* (Cambridge, Mass., 1973), p. 2: "Mental illness epitomizes social disintegration."

18. 9 *St. Comm. Lun.* 1914, p. 17; 6 *St. Bd. Char. and Corr.* 1915, p. 33; 12 *St. Comm. Lun.* 1920, p. 7.

and have even more extended plans for next season." The *San Francisco Call* reported on one impending military maneuver—a mock skirmish between "American" and "Spanish" troops complete with a charge up San Juan Hill—and noted that "the public is welcome to attend this unusual spectacle." Several thousand visitors turned out, proving that the eighteenth-century practice of putting "madmen" on display for the entertainment of normal people was not yet completely dead.[19]

Among those sample members committed to state hospitals from San Francisco, "refusal to work" or "inability to work" was cited in seventeen cases as a "fact indicating insanity." In 1914, for example, an 18-year-old girl was committed on her mother's recommendation because she was "abusive at home, stays out 'til 1 or 2 A.M., and refuses to work." A 35-year-old ironworker, accused by his wife in 1916, was sent to a state hospital because he "talks of Eddyism [Christian Science], quit his work in order to investigate things"—an action that was particularly irrational from the medical standpoint since it marked a conversion to a non-medical form of therapy. Another blue-collar worker was committed in 1918 on the sole grounds that he "was a defective from early youth, couldn't get along in school, later on preferred to be hanging around street corners; wouldn't work during last three to four years." The German socialist baker cited earlier not only had "unlimited nerve getting on without work," but "states that people are fools to work."

In other cases the refusal to work figured implicitly in the judgment of insanity. A 50-year-old housewife, for

19. 5 *St. Bd. Char. and Corr.* 1912, p. 34; 12 *St. Comm. Lun.* 1920, p. 7; 8 *St. Bd. Char. and Corr.* 1918, p. 59; Dr. Leonard Stocking, "Report of the Medical Superintendent," 8 *St. Comm. Lun.* 1912, p. 59; "Army of Madmen to Meet on Battlefield," *San Francisco Call*, August 29, 1912, p. 4; "Army of Insane in Line for War," *Call*, August 31, 1912, p. 10; "San Jose Holds Military Pageant," *Call*, September 3, 1912, p. 7.

instance, was committed in 1920 after her husband testified that she was "unable to concentrate her mind on any of her household duties." But the largest number of such cases were the vagrants. Fifteen sample members were committed primarily on the grounds that they were vagrant tramps—a social group that included, according to the State Board of Charities and Corrections, a "large number" of "morons."[20]

In 1906, for instance, the court committed a 47-year-old Scotsman, who "has been in the country six months, about all of which has been spent in the County Jail for vagrancy." His only other "symptom" was that he "appears stupid . . . poor memory." In 1914 another man with a "poor memory"—a 45-year-old widowed carpenter—was declared insane after being "arrested on complaint of people who objected to his being about a public park in his filthy condition."

A 21-year-old Chinese man—whose religion, the examiner noted, was "Confusionist"—was arrested for vagrancy in 1925. "Unable to answer questions intelligently or explain himself or state where he lived," he was taken to the Detention Hospital, whereupon he "became violent, was placed in full restraint." Three days after his arrest, the vagrancy charge was dismissed and he was committed to Napa. In 1926, a 49-year-old Italian-born laborer, who "is a public charge, fed by Salvation Army," was "picked up by police" and commit-

20. 6 *St. Bd. Char. and Corr.* 1915, p. 33. It is important to note that the relatively new category "moron," like that of the "imbecile," was entirely based upon a concept of productivity in the marketplace. An imbecile was "capable of guarding himself against common physical danger," but was "incapable of earning his own living"; a "moron," on the other hand, could earn a living "under favorable circumstances," but was "incapable of competing on equal terms with his normal fellows or managing himself and his own affairs with ordinary prudence." The Board of Charities proceeded to point out that more than 75 percent of "the inmates of jails, reformatories, and penitentiaries," and 50 percent of "the women engaged in public prostitution" were "imbeciles," 6 *St. Bd. Char. and Corr.* 1915, pp. 32-33.

ted on their recommendation. He was reported to be "unable to give a clear account of himself, doesn't seem to understand questions asked, nor does he give rational answers"—not surprising, one might suppose, in view of his inability to understand the questions. Like those persons who "refused to work," the vagrants were visible, bothersome "rebels" against what Christopher Lasch has called "the single standard of honor" in a bourgeois society: the duty to be self-reliant, independent, productive.[21]

"The terrible plague of vagabondage," as the world's most renowned clinical psychiatrist, Emil Kraepelin, declared, could not be arrested "by means of the panacea of short terms of imprisonment, or that much-dreaded punishment, committal to the penal work house." Long-term detention and treatment were the answer.[22] Of course, only the most bothersome of the vagrants—a tiny proportion of the vagrant population—were ever committed; financial considerations alone prevented a mass confinement. It is important to stress, however, that those explicit deviants committed for vagrancy were confined not because they were in fact mentally incapacitated or destructive, but because they represented noncompliance with the cultural norm of productive efficiency; they were troubling, and ultimately intolerable, because they refused to work.

Moreover, the San Francisco commitment records show that even some residual deviants were in fact judged to be in need of treatment because they would not work. Of course many aged persons committed for

21. Lasch, "Origins of the Asylum," *The World of Nations*, p. 17.

22. Dr. Emil Kraepelin, *Lectures on Clinical Psychiatry*, 3rd English ed. (London, 1913), pp. 524-525. Two important articles on the history of vagrancy are Bronislaw Geremak, "Criminalité, vagabondage, paupérisme: la marginalité à l'aube des temps modernes," *Revue d'histoire moderne et contemporaine* 21 (juillet-septembre 1974), 337-375, and William J. Chambliss, "A Sociological Analysis of the Law of Vagrancy," *Social Problems* 12 (Spring 1964), 67-77.

insanity probably became intolerable to their families not because of behavioral idiosyncrasies alone, but because they were unable to contribute their share to family "production." The stability of bourgeois social order—as Durkheim suggested—may still have been dependent in the early twentieth century upon the institutionalization of these and other explicit deviants, such as alcoholics, drug addicts, criminals, and juvenile delinquents. Ritually expelled and yet still dramatically visible in their fortress-style asylums, the insane were a permanent sign of where vital social boundaries lay.

IV

The concept of insanity had been closely linked with "mental illness" through the late nineteenth century, in both the popular and the professional mind. By the early twentieth century, however, this connection was clearly disappearing: mental illness was increasingly distinct from insanity. The "mentally ill" might often, despite their affliction, be functioning members of the community; their "sickness" was neither, of necessity, incapacitating nor chronic. The "insane," on the other hand, were all the more clearly recognized as disruptive, bothersome, unproductive; like outright criminals, they were in need of both corrective treatment and detention.

In fact, the insane had always had a great deal in common with criminals, despite efforts by nineteenth-century humanitarian reformers to segregate the two groups into separate institutions. Prior to the nineteenth century, the insane were commonly grouped with other offenders.[23] Yet even after specialized insane asylums emerged, "criminal" treatment persisted. Like regular lawbreakers, the insane were "arrested," brought to a local detention center, judged in a court, transported to

23. Lasch, "Origins of the Asylum," p. 9; Gerald N. Grob, *Mental Institutions in America* (New York, 1973), p. 13; Albert Deutsch, *The Mentally Ill in America* (New York, 1937), pp. 39-54.

their institution by a sheriff, and involuntarily confined. The major difference between the two cases was that while the sentence of the criminal was limited to a stated period of time, that of the insane person was indeterminate. Indeed, penal reformers and penitentiary wardens looked with envy upon the indeterminacy of state hospital commitments, and argued that the system made sense for prisons too. For, as the State Board of Charities and Corrections urged in 1916, "law violators are a sort of sick folk to be treated until cured, or if incurable, to be continuously restrained." Determining sentences on the basis of the alleged "criminality of the act" ignored the fact that "some persons who never have committed serious crimes should be permanently segregated." As with the insane, "corrective treatment . . . should be based on the character of the offender instead of on the nature of the particular act for which he was arrested."[24]

The insane commitment procedure was a system of indefinitely confining, on grounds of "character," not only those who had committed no serious crimes, but those who had committed no crimes at all. Many of those sentenced to prison terms were acknowledged to be "just like" the insane, except for their explicit transgression of a law. As the psychiatrist William A. White asserted, "A large number of the so-called criminals are so merely by accident, and, if they had not happened to have done something which ran counter to a statute, their path would in all probability have led to a hospital for the insane."[25] What the State Board of Charities and Corrections was calling for was simply an explicit recognition of that fact: many "criminals" were defectives in need not of sentencing, but of segregating.

The persistence of "criminal" treatment of the insane in early twentieth-century California is especially evident in the detention facilities provided at the county level

24. 7 *St. Bd. Char. and Corr.* 1916, p. 53.
25. Dr. William A. White, cited in "Passing of 'Insanity,'" 616.

and in the transportation-by-sheriff system. Beginning in 1897, the Lunacy Law of the state provided expressly that "no person alleged to be insane shall be associated with criminals, or those charged with or convicted of crime." Yet the practice of indiscriminately grouping criminals and the alleged insane continued in many sections of the state. In 1920, 29 of 58 California counties still confined them in the same jail cells.[26] Even those counties, like San Francisco, that erected separate detention hospitals for the alleged insane had in fact provided only an additional jail with a euphemistic label. The San Francisco facility—complete with locked cells—was in 1916 "a jail in all but name," according to an investigator for the New York Bureau of Municipal Research. A survey in 1930 repeated that observation: the San Francisco Detention Hospital was a "hospital in which the jail atmosphere has been reproduced." In addition, the survey noted that in the state as a whole, 28 counties out of the 46 surveyed "detain mental patients in jails only," and 17 others—like San Francisco—provided only a "jail-like facility."[27]

The transporting of the insane to state hospitals by sheriff's deputies was another nineteenth-century tradition that would not die—despite repeated protests of state hospital and charity officials. From its inception, the State Board of Charities and Corrections insisted that insanity must be "decriminalized" by eliminating the sheriff's role. Hospital superintendents also decried the practice, claiming that patients who might otherwise have been cured were rendered incurable by the sheriff's use of restraint during the trip.[28]

But even while they were attempting to decriminalize

26. 1 *St. Comm. Lun.* 1899, p. 6; 9 *St. Bd. Char. and Corr.* 1922, p. 33.

27. Bureau of Municipal Research, *Survey of the Government of San Francisco*, p. 471; Allen, *Mental Hygiene Survey*, pp. 138-139.

28. 1 *St. Bd. Char. and Corr.* 1905, pp. 36-37; 2 *St. Bd. Char. and Corr.* 1906, pp. 63-65; 7 *St. Bd. Char. and Corr.* 1916, p. 37.

insanity, state officials were willing to grant that "an insane person is a dangerous person in the community." As long as the insane were widely considered to be dangerous to be at large, legislators would vote to keep them in the sheriff's hands until they were behind locked doors.[29] The sheriffs maintained their position in the commitment process not only because they were themselves an organized lobby—eager to protect a safe, lucrative part of their job, one that the *Call* termed the sheriff's "petty transportation graft"—but because the identification in the popular mind between the criminal and the insane remained close.[30]

It would appear in fact that in the early twentieth century a "reintegration" of deviant roles was taking place. Although they were still institutionally segregated from one another, the insane, the criminal, the alcoholic, and the delinquent were all coming to be viewed as both "sick" and "dangerous" and for that reason in need of corrective treatment and indefinite confinement. In the eighteenth century such deviants had been commonly lumped together both institutionally and intellectually. In the nineteenth century the "sick" deviants—the insane—were segregated from the "well," those who were mentally "normal," rational, in possession of their full capacities.

But by the early twentieth century the distinction between the mentally normal and the mentally abnormal was breaking down. "Even normal persons," wrote Dr.

---

29. 2 *St. Bd. Char. and Corr.* 1906, p. 64. The State Board introduced legislation to end the sheriff transporation system in 1921, but it was defeated. 10 *St. Bd. Char. and Corr.* 1923, p. 22.

30. "Gross Cruelty to the Insane," *San Francisco Call,* June 11, 1911, p. 32. The State Board of Charities was equally blunt. "It is only fair to say that the reason this system has continued is that it involves a fee of five dollars per day for the sheriff." 7 *St. Bd. Char. and Corr.* 1916, p. 37. "The effort to have state hospital attendants transport insane patients is always blocked by the sheriff's lobby which sees in it the loss of fees and perquisites of office." "Conduct of Insanity Proceedings," 10 *California Law Review* 227 (1922).

John Haynes of the State Board of Charities and Corrections in 1918, "are seldom free from a trace, at least, of hereditary nerve defect." In the first years of the century "the concept of mental illness," as William A. White later emphasized, "was being enlarged to include a great many things besides the types that we were accustomed to see in public institutions. Not only were the minor psychoses and the neuroses included, but all forms of social maladjustment and even unhappiness were seen to have mechanisms quite the same as the more serious conditions with which we were more familiar."[31] As a consequence, deviants of whatever type came to be seen as sharing a single, basic characteristic—that of being "defective." What distinguished criminals from the insane was no longer their "rationality" but their explicit breaking of the law. As a *New York Times* editorial entitled "The Criminal as Patient" put it in 1925, "one-quarter of the jail population is approximately normal in body and mind. . . . But the remaining three-quarters were invalids before they were criminals. . . . With proper treatment in time the first offender stands a good chance of becoming a useful member of society."[32]

Moreover, deviants as a group were to be distinguished from nondeviants not by their mental condition, but by their inability to function effectively as members

31. Dr. John R. Haynes, "Sterilization," 8 *St. Bd. Char. and Corr.* 1918, p. 62; William A. White, "The Origin, Growth, and Significance of the Mental Hygiene Movement," in Williams, ed., *Proceedings of the First International Congress of Mental Hygiene*, p. 527.

32. "The Criminal as Patient," Editorial, *New York Times*, July 14, 1925, p. 20. On the emerging tendency to interpret juvenile delinquency as "disease," see Robert H. Bremner, ed., *Children and Youth in America: A Documentary History*, vol. 2 (Cambridge, Mass., 1971), pp. 555-576. On the emergence of alcoholism as a disease, see Craig MacAndrew, "On the Notion that Certain Persons Who Are Given to Frequent Drunkenness Suffer from a Disease Called Alcoholism," in Stanley C. Plog and Robert B. Edgerton, eds., *Changing Perspectives in Mental Illness* (New York, 1969), pp. 483-501.

of the community. Effective functioning, not the absence of mental or nervous disorder, became the prime criterion of "normality." The insane came to constitute that group of unproductive, bothersome defectives who, though they had committed no crime, required an indefinite and involuntary program of "treatment" and confinement. The "mentally ill," on the other hand, were those moderately disturbed individuals whose productive potential had not yet been undermined.

The new spirit of toleration and sympathy toward the mentally ill in the early twentieth century appears to have helped legitimize the prolonged detention of the insane. For the insane could now be viewed as that group of deviants who had been given the opportunity to respond to the sophisticated treatment available in urban psychopathic wards; if the most talented medical and psychiatric professionals were unable to cure their disorder, then there was truly no alternative to custodial care. The establishment of psychopathic wards—the partial result of public demands for easy access to psychiatric treatment—made it easier at the same time for physicians to commit the insane to state hospitals. Not only did the psychopathic ward in practice eliminate the court hearing, but it offered clinically authoritative judgments that non-experts were in no position to doubt.

Despite, therefore, the emergence of a new concept of mental illness, of a more sympathetic attitude toward the mentally ill who were willing to enter a therapeutic relationship, and of new urban institutions for the treatment of acute cases, the system of involuntary, indefinite commitments to state hospitals was preserved, even strengthened. Insane hospitals continued in the early twentieth century to perform the same social function they had begun to perform in the late eighteenth: the visible "marking" of the "irrational" or otherwise "abnormal" persons who, as Foucault has argued, implicitly rendered their negative witness to the power of cultural norms. The state subsidized the custodial, often lifetime, care of those who would not, or could not, observe the fundamental social rules to which "normal" adults consciously or unconsciously subscribed.

Appendix

Each San Francisco civil commitment record contained six parts: (1) the original petition accusing the individual of insanity (The Affidavit of Insanity); (2) the Warrant of Arrest; (3) the Order Fixing Time for Hearing and Examination; (4) the Certificate of Medical Examiners; (5) the Judgment of Insanity and Order of Commitment of Insane Person; and (6) the Statement of Financial Ability. Each case record filled four large folio pages (10 by 18 inches). The longest section was the Certificate of Medical Examiners, which contained the following questions:

Social Background Information

Name.
Address.
Age.
Nativity.
If foreign-born, from what part or place did (s)he come to the United States, and when and where did (s)he land?
How long in California?
Place from which he came to this State.
Sex.
Color.
Occupation.
Religious Belief.

Education.

Civil Condition [Marital Status].

If female and married, give maiden name.

Maiden Name of Mother.

Number of Children of Mother, Living and Dead.

Has either parent been addicted to the use of opium, cocaine, tobacco, or alcoholic beverages to excess, or other stimulating narcotics?

Have any relatives been eccentric or peculiar in anyway in their habits or pursuits? If so how?

Which parent does alleged insane person resemble mentally? Physically?

Has alleged insane person ever been addicted to masturbation or sexual excesses? If so, for how long?

State alleged insane person's habits as to use of liquor, tobacco, opium, or other drugs, and whether excessive or moderate.

What is alleged insane person's natural disposition or temperament, and mental capacity?

Has alleged insane person insane relatives? If so, state the degree of consanguinity, and whether paternal or maternal.

Medical History

What is alleged insane person's general physical condition?

Specify any disease of which alleged insane person has suffered, or does suffer, or any injury received.

Have any relatives, direct or collateral, suffered, or are they suffering, from any form of chronic disease, such as consumption or tuberculosis, syphilis, rheumatism, neuralgia, hysteria, or nervousness, or had epilepsy or falling sickness?

Has alleged insane person ever had convulsions? If so, when did (s)he have the first one? When the last one?

Has alleged insane person ever been an inmate of an institution for the insane? If so, state when, where, and how long. Whether discharged or otherwise.

Number of previous attacks.

Date of previous attacks.

Length of time each previous attack lasted.

Present attack began [date].

Was the present attack gradual or rapid in its onset?

Is alleged insane person noisy, restless, violent, dangerous, destructive, incendiary, excited or depressed?

Homicidal or suicidal? (If either homicide or suicide has been attempted or threatened, it should be so stated.)

Age when menses appeared. Amount and character before insanity appeared. Since insanity appeared.

Has the change of life taken place? Was it gradual or sudden? How changed from normal?

Memory.

Sleep.

Headache or neuralgia.

Constipation or indigestion.

Hallucinations.

Delusions. (Specify, if possible, and whether fixed or changeable.)

What is the supposed cause of insanity? Predisposing. Exciting.

Other facts indicating insanity. (State what the alleged insane person said and did in the presence of the examiners, and how changed in business or social habits, and disposition, as communicated to examiners by others.)

What treatment has been pursued? (State remedies given, and whether hypodermically or not.)

Whether patient has been restrained by muff, belt, or otherwise.

DIAGNOSIS:

Note on Sources

A longer bibliography of works consulted in the research for this book may be found in my dissertation, "Madness in Urban America: A Social and Cultural Study of Commitments for Insanity in San Francisco, 1906-1929" (Stanford, 1975). This note will mention only the most significant primary sources; the footnotes contain references to the remaining primary sources and to many of the secondary materials.

The key sources for this book were the 63 volumes of *Records of Commitments for Insanity* (May 1906 to May 1929) and the four volumes of *Records of Examination of Alleged Insane Persons and Orders of Discharge from Detention Hospital* (March 1909 to April 1929), San Francisco Superior Court. Until 1977 these records, along with a rich but disorganized collection of other city and county documents (especially probate and police records), were located at the San Francisco City and County Records Center, and were freely accessible to any researcher with enough patience to hunt for them. All of these materials are now located at the Bekins Storage Facility, Masonic Avenue and Geary Blvd., San Francisco, where they are for the first time being classified. Access to the documents, unfortunately, now appears to be restricted.

Another useful manuscript source was the Minute Books of the San Francisco Board of Health, which are indexed by subject for the early twentieth century and available at the Accounting Office, San Francisco Department of Public Health. The Minute Books provided a vital glimpse of off-the-record discussions among city officials and physicians on the

190

subjects of the treatment of the alleged insane and the psychopathic ward, from the 1910s through the 1920s.

Municipal, state, and federal government publications were indispensable, both for their wealth of statistical data and for their often detailed accounts of institutional life, of bureaucratic procedures in the management of deviants, and of policy debates among officials and reformers. San Francisco's *Municipal Reports* (1867-1917), available at the Stanford, University of California at Berkeley, and San Francisco Public libraries, brought together in one annual volume the reports of all city departments for most of the years covered by this book. After 1917, the County Clerk—who was responsible for keeping track of examinations, commitments, and discharges —continued to issue an annual report under separate cover; unfortunately, the Board of Health (renamed the Department of Public Health in 1923) did not continue to issue annual reports, with the exception of one for the single fiscal year 1924-1925. Apparently only one copy of that report, located at the Stanford University library, is extant.

At the state level, the most important publications for my purposes were the *Biennial Report of the State Commission in Lunacy* (1898-1920) and its successor, the State Department of Institutions (1923-1930); and the *Biennial Report of the State Board of Charities and Corrections* (1903-1923) and its successors, the State Department of Public Welfare (1927) and the State Department of Social Welfare (1929). Each report contained invaluable statistical material as well as a variety of topical essays, graphic accounts of institutional operations, and repeated proposals for reform. The State Board of Charities and Corrections, as befitted its initial "watchdog" role, was more often critical of state practices in dealing with the insane and the alleged insane than was the State Commission in Lunacy, the agency directly responsible for administering California's asylums. But both sets of reports provided valuable insight into the thinking of medical and judicial authorities, legislators, and reformers, and contained otherwise unobtainable statewide statistical data. The published transcripts of the *Proceedings* of the California State Conference of Charities and Corrections (1904, 1906,

1909, 1911) offered verbatim debates between state medical officials, private physicians, and assorted reformers—debates that often contained blunter statements of opinion than those given in the more staid reports of the State Board or the State Commission. For the late nineteenth century the annual or biennial reports of the individual asylums (in some years combined with the report of the State Board of Health) are the only source of statistical information on commitments for insanity, and those data are meager. But the reports are essential for grasping the function that asylums performed from their beginnings in the 1850s—the function of detaining and furnishing minimal custodial care to disturbing though sane individuals, a practice against which many asylum superintendents protested vehemently in their reports. Virtually full runs of all state documents relating to the insane are located at the California State Library in Sacramento, and all but a few can be found in the Stanford, University of California at Berkeley, and San Francisco Public libraries.

The most important federal documents were published by the Bureau of the Census, Department of Commerce (until 1903 known as the Census Office, Department of the Interior). In addition to the indispensable decennial *Population* reports, the Bureau published several other excellent volumes. The *Report on the Defective, Dependent, and Delinquent Classes* (Washington, D.C., 1888), *Report on the Insane, Feeble-Minded, Deaf and Dumb, and Blind in the United States* (Washington, D.C., 1895), *Insane and Feeble-Minded in Institutions, 1904* (Washington, D.C., 1905), and *Insane and Feeble-Minded in Institutions, 1910* (Washington, 1914)— based respectively on the Tenth through Thirteenth Censuses —were particularly significant because of their efforts to analyze nationwide trends in hospitalization for insanity. They supplied many clues for the treatment of the San Francisco data in Chapter Five. Other useful Census reports (all published in Washington, D.C., in the years given in parentheses) included *Benevolent Institutions, 1904* (1905), *Benevolent Institutions, 1910* (1913), *Paupers in Almshouses, 1904* (1906), *Paupers in Almshouses, 1910* (1915), *Summary of Laws Relating to the Dependent Classes, 1913* (1914), *Statistical Directory of State Institutions for the Defective,*

Dependent, and Delinquent Classes, 1915-1916 (1919), *Patients in Hospitals for Mental Disease* (1926), and *Mental Patients in State Hospitals, 1926-1927* (1930).

Congressional investigations of immigration in the early twentieth century devoted considerable attention to the alleged disproportion of foreigners among the insane—a view simultaneously rejected by the Census Bureau's 1910 report on the insane and feebleminded. For the Congressional viewpoint see especially "Pauperism and Insanity," 57th Congress, 1st Session, *Reports of the Industrial Commission on Immigration and Education*, Vol. XV (Washington, D.C., 1901), pp. LXX-LXXIII, and "Immigration and Insanity," 61st Congress, 3rd Session, *Abstracts of Reports of the Immigration Commission*, Vol. 2 (Washington, D.C., 1911) pp. 227-251.

Among nongovernmental bodies organized at the national level, the many publications of the National Committee for Mental Hygiene—especially its journal *Mental Hygiene* (which I consulted for the years 1917-1930)—and the annual transcripts of the *Proceedings* of the National Conference of Charities and Corrections (1874-1916), and its successor the National Conference of Social Work (1917-1930), were particularly important.

San Francisco newspapers were a source of vital information about particular events, personalities, and institutions, and contained many revealing editorials on insanity, on the medical, legal, and psychiatric professions, and on state institutions. Fortunately the three major dailies—the *Call*, the *Chronicle*, and the *Examiner*—are fully indexed by subject for the years 1904 through 1949. That superb index is in card form at the California State Library, Sacramento. In addition, the State Library has a bound, two-volume index to the *Call* for the years 1894-1903 (microfilm edition at the Bancroft Library, University of California at Berkeley) and a somewhat haphazard subject index to nineteenth-century publications that includes references to insanity in the *Daily Alta California* for the 1850s and the *Morning Call* for the 1880s.

Among the professional medical and psychiatric journals that I consulted for the years before 1930, the most helpful by far were the *American Journal of Insanity* (1870-1921) and its successor the *American Journal of Psychiatry* (1921-1930).

Others that were occasionally useful include the *Journal of Mental and Nervous Diseases* (1876-1930), *Alienist and Neurologist* (1880-1920), *Archives of Neurology and Psychiatry* (1919-1930), *Archives of Occupational Therapy* (1922-1930), *California and Western Medicine* (1924-1930), *Hospital Social Service* (1919-1930), *Journal of Sociologic Medicine* (1915-1928), *Medico-Legal Journal* (1883-1930), *Modern Hospital* (1913-1930), *Pacific Medical and Surgical Journal* (1870-1917), *Psychiatric Quarterly* (1927-1930), and *State Hospital Quarterly* (1915-1927).

Index

Act to Prevent the Overcrowding of Asylums (1885), 43

Adams, George S., 58n

Age and social characteristics of insane, 87, 105, 107-108, 109, 110, 114, 118, 128-129, 131-134, 138-139, 160

Aged, and insanity, 94-95, 125, 131-134, 138-139, 159, 160, 179-180; and Irish, 92-95. *See also* Old Age; Senility

Agnews (San Jose) State Hospital, 57, 81, 82

Alcoholism, 123, 130, 139n-140n, 142, 144, 154, 155, 159, 161, 183, 184n. *See also* Intemperance

Allen, Frederick H., 76n

Almshouses, 19n, 44; for old and destitute men, 131-132

American Psychiatric Association, 158

Anderson, Nels, 5

Anomie, 5

Anti-immigration movement, 105-106, 109-110

Ariès, Philippe, 90n

"Asexualization." *See* Sterilization

Asian, 92, 94, 96, 157

Asylums for the insane: bed capacity of public and private, in California, 116-117; in bourgeois society, 11-13, 185-186; called "hospitals," 54n; custodial function of, 14-15, 17-18, 41-47, 60n; in early and mid-1800s, 7-14; in late 1800s and early 1900s, 17-18; length of stay at, 81n; moral treatment at, 14-15, 17-18; municipal, 60n; overcrowding at, 21-22, 25-26, 28, 43, 46-47, 75, 76; rural, 58-59; as shelter for elderly women, 132, 133-134, 160; and social control, 7-14; superintendents critical of custodial function of, 41-47

Australians, 73

Banner, James, 8n

Barr, Martin W., 33

Barrett, Albert M., 71n

Beard, George M., 170

Beers, Clifford, 170

Bittner, Egon, 86n, 129n

Bloombaum, M., 157n

Blue-collar workers as insane: behavior of, reported by medical examiners, 153, 155, 157; social characteristics, 21, 88, 105, 112-117, 127, 128

Bourgeois society: canons of normality in, 149-150; insanity in, 13-14, 174-175, 185-186

Brandt, Anthony, 2n

Bremner, Robert H., 184n

Brenner, M. Harvey, 176n

Burnham, John C., 3, 169

Composition	University of California Press
Lithography	Thomson-Shore, Inc.
Binder	Thomson-Shore, Inc.
Text	Compset 500 Garamond
Display	Compset 500 Garamond
Paper	50 lb P & S Offset Vellum B-32
Binding	Kivar 5 Black Kidskin